CW00554140

EXERCISE
TIGER

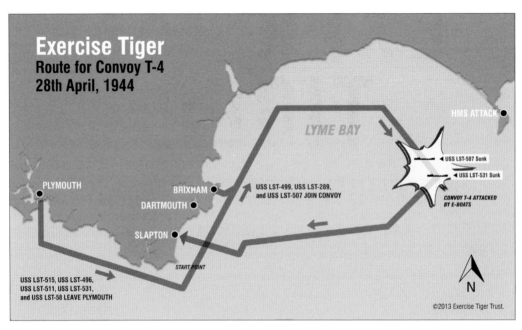

Map showing the route of Convoy T-4 and the E-boat attack site. *Map courtesy of Exercise Tiger Trust*

EXERCISE TIGER

TIGER

THE FORGOTTEN SACRIFICE
OF THE SILENT FEW

WENDY LAWRANCE

FONTHILL

Fonthill Media Limited
Fonthill Media LLC
www.fonthillmedia.com
office@fonthillmedia.com

First published in the United Kingdom 2013

British Library Cataloguing in Publication Data:

A catalogue record for this book is available from the British Library

Copyright © Wendy Lawrance 2013

ISBN 978-1-78155-110-3

The right of Wendy Lawrance to be identified as the author of this work has been asserted by
him in accordance with the Copyright, Designs and Patents Act 1988.

All rights reserved. No part of this publication may be reproduced, stored in a retrieval system
or transmitted in any form or by any means, electronic, mechanical, photocopying, recording or
otherwise, without prior permission in writing from Fonthill Media Limited

Typeset in Sabon 10/13
Printed and bound in England

Connect with us

 facebook.com/fonthillmedia  twitter.com/fonthillmedia

Contents

Acknowledgements

Back in 2007, my husband, Steve and I were asked to become trustees of the only UK charity which commemorates Exercise Tiger; The Exercise Tiger Trust. Our first task was to go through the documents and materials held by the previous Trustees. This took several months of collating and cataloguing at which point, we both had a much clearer perspective on the exercise and its aftermath. After this, our next job was to decide what to do with the charity itself and, after much deliberation, we decided that the previous incumbent's ambition to build a 'wall of names' was unrealistic and—to a certain extent—unnecessary. Instead, we chose to create an online roll of honour. However, we did not want to just provide a list of names, so I set about investigating every single individual who had perished and, using the casualty lists provided by the American Battle Monuments Commission, I was able to trace each one of the men who died on that night and discovered as much as I could about them. As a result of those painstaking months of research, the roll of honour provided on the Exercise Tiger Trust website is, probably, the most comprehensive and detailed memorial to those who gave their lives that night. We believe that, in this way, anyone, from anywhere in the world, can access and discover the details and information about these men, without having to travel or leave the comfort of their own home, thus making the whole event more accessible.

We made it our policy, from the beginning, to present the documents, where possible, as they were given to us, not to cloud them with judgements or political agendas, but to allow those who were interested to read them to come to their own verdict, based on the evidence placed before them. We remain, to this day, impartial.

When I was approached to write this book, I decided that I was not going to write yet another book propounding the conspiracies and cover-ups which have come to dominate this story in recent years. In common with the policy of the Trust, I have chosen, instead to present a series of facts. That said, I have offered some opinion at the end of this book and that focused around my personal perspective of those who seek to further their own status by creating intrigue where there is none. For most of the claims made, a perfectly logical explanation can be found, but it must be said that logical explanations do not sell books, or create reputations.

There are many people who have helped me, directly and indirectly, with the writing of this book. First and foremost I would like to acknowledge and thank all those writers who have gone before me, specifically Nigel Lewis, whose book *Channel Firing: The Tragedy of Exercise Tiger* is an invaluable resource to anyone wishing to understand this event. Although he was not the first to bring Exercise Tiger to the public eye, his rational perspective has done a great deal to help with the genuine understanding of what happened.

The first-hand accounts given by the survivors of the E-boat attack have provided crucial details and information, enabling real eye-witness perspective on the event. While they vary in accuracy, and particulars, their content is strikingly evocative of that brief moment in time. In particular, the accounts provided by Eugene Eckstam, Patsy Giacchi and Angelo Crapanzano have been indispensable in the creation of this book.

I would like to offer my thanks to Jason Free, a Patron of the Exercise Tiger Trust for his research carried out in America on my behalf, as well as his unfailing support. I would also like to thank my fellow Trustees Malcolm Crow, Dominic Ford and, especially, my husband, Steve Lawrance, who has been so supportive during the writing of this book.

Finally, the utmost respect and honour goes to the men who served not only in Exercise Tiger, but in all the exercises, and operations during the Second World War, many of whom are no longer with us. Their willingness to commit to their countries and families should be a lesson to those of us who have continued to benefit from their sacrifices.

Author's Note

My main aim in this project, other than to raise funds for the charity, was to produce an account of the event which was accessible to all, so that everyone who takes an interest would be able to understand it, with the minimum of technical embellishment. I have, therefore, kept the specialist data to a minimum, creating—hopefully—a more personal story what happened. A 'Who's Who' and the Technical Specifications for the ships is supplied separately at the end of the book, rather than being included in the text, for ease of reference.

For the same reason and to make the text easier to read, rather than providing footnotes, I have simply listed the sources for each chapter at the end of the book.

For further information about Exercise Tiger please visit The Exercise Tiger Trust website at www.exercisetiger.org.uk

'Long Ago and Far Away'

Exercise Tiger was one of a series of military exercises which took place off the coast of south Devon, involving American soldiers and sailors as part of their preparations for the D-Day landings, during the early months of 1944. To many (but not all) of these exercises were attached the code names of animals, such as 'Fox', 'Beaver', 'Muskrat', 'Otter' and 'Mink'. Other names were significantly more obscure, like Exercises 'Chevrolet', 'Jalopy', 'Snipe' and 'Cellophane'. Almost without exception, though, these training exercises have long since been forgotten—as is quite natural for a relatively uneventful series of practice operations in which men were trained in various aspects of amphibious landings. Exercise Tiger would have gone the same way and become another overlooked and brief moment among so many, were it not for one thing: on the second night of the exercise, over 600 men lost their lives during a German E-boat attack. That event and its aftermath changed the lives of thousands of people for many decades and caused a series of controversies that would echo down the years.

Depending on which source you look at, somewhere between 25,000 and 30,000 men took part in Exercise Tiger as a whole and on the night of 28th April, several thousand of these men were occupying eight LSTs (Landing Ships, Tank) *en route* from either Brixham or Plymouth, to Slapton Sands. When the E-boats attacked, a large percentage of the men on board witnessed and survived the E-boat attack. Over 600 of their number did not, however and, taking into account the dead, their bereaved families, the wounded, traumatised, witnesses and survivors, this event has touched the lives of probably tens of thousands of people. Since that night, a fair amount has been written about what happened, but despite this, it remains a relatively obscure episode of the Second World War. To those US servicemen who participated, or others who witnessed the E-boat attack and its aftermath it was, of course, momentous, but to many others, it remains either mysterious, or completely unheard of.

The local villagers who were evacuated from their homes in and around the area of Slapton Sands for the duration of all the exercises, recall packing up their belongings, their time away from home and their eventual return to their villages many months later. However, at the time, almost none of them had any idea of the tragedy that had taken place on their doorstep in their absence. They found out about it later and a memorial was erected; a local man, Ken Small, salvaged a tank from one of the earlier exercises and this stands near the beach in memory of the men who lost their lives. At the time, however, nothing was said.

To the wider public in Great Britain, Exercise Tiger means almost nothing to this day. Its story has occasionally featured in television documentaries, although these are usually made with the purpose of sensationalising, rather than informing. In 2008, the events of the E-boat attack featured in an episode of the ITV drama *Foyle's War*, but whether the audience appreciated that this was a genuine historical event, rather than a piece of television fiction, is debatable. Whenever I inform people that I am one of the trustees of the only UK-based charity which commemorates the event (The Exercise Tiger Trust), they do seem to assume that my role has something to do with the preservation or conservation of a large cat species. When the true purpose of the charity is explained, the response is invariably surprise that so little is known about something so tragic.

In America, while there is a little more understanding about Exercise Tiger and there are several not-for-profit organisations set up to commemorate the victims, it still remains a topic that is rarely, if ever, discussed or used as a topic in documentaries or films, or covered within the realms of education. Although this might seem surprising, considering the number of casualties involved and the scale of the disaster, there are very good reasons for its anonymity.

Firstly, the men (and some women) involved, whether they were military personnel, or doctors and nurses who treated the wounded, were ordered to maintain a strict silence over everything that had occurred, some of them under the threat of court martial. For some of these men, this imposed silence would be life-long, or certainly it would last for many decades, partially perhaps because no-one ever officially gave them leave to speak of it. At the same time, however, a great many of the survivors simply did not want to talk about their traumatic experiences, as is quite common with the survivors of such events.

The main reason behind this urgent need for secrecy was the imminent arrival of D-Day itself. Two of the purposes in selecting Slapton Sands as the site for these exercises were the similarity between that stretch of South Devon coast and the Normandy beaches, as well as the fact that the real sites for the D-Day preparations and collection of assets were some distance away. It was hoped, therefore, that even if the Germans did manage to find out about the exercises, they would not realise their significance and would not be able to do any damage to the equipment which was being gathered in readiness for the invasion. The deaths of so many men in the E-boat attack, which showed that the Allies were practising something involving the amphibious landing of large numbers of troops and their necessary equipment, was an absolute giveaway that the exercises at Slapton were important to the invasion and the enemy might then have been able to ascertain the destination of the invading forces. It was imperative, therefore, that absolute secrecy should be maintained until after the Normandy landings had taken place.

Some have argued that this order for silence was unreasonable and that the tones in which it was made were threatening, but at the time, the military authorities were most concerned that their plans for D-Day—which had been many months in the making—should not be ruined by someone speaking carelessly or out of turn. It had taken so long to pull together the necessary number of men and equipment, which were being corralled all across Southern England ready to cross the Channel: to have to change the plans with only forty days to go until D-Day would have caused untold delays and would probably have lengthened the war, ultimately costing many more lives.

Another reason why no-one really knows very much about Exercise Tiger is, quite simply, its timing. D-Day, with its numerous casualties and far-reaching consequences for the outcome of the war, simply overtook the more minor events that had come before it. In terms of casualties, while Exercise Tiger's E-boat attack was costly, the landings at Utah beach, for which Tiger was a rehearsal, actually claimed less than half the lives of the E-boat attack. This might seem like a reason for focusing on Exercise Tiger in a commemorative fashion. However, the bloody experiences of Omaha beach overshadowed everything else, resulting in more casualties than the other four landing sites put together and, thereby, fixing itself as a foremost event in American war history.

As the seventieth anniversary of the Exercise approaches, there will perhaps be an increase in the interest shown in this tragic event, although it will almost certainly be overshadowed again by the D-Day commemorations which will take place in the following months. Some—especially the families of the men who died and those who returned—will remember and pause to take a moment to think about what happened that night. For the men who survived the disaster, almost none of whom remain to tell their stories, there were never really any special anniversary days or commemorations, although several veterans did make the emotional journey back to Slapton Sands to remember their fallen comrades. For the survivors, it was not just 28th April, but every day that brought a memory, a flashback or a sad thought and every night came the dreams or—worse still—the nightmares of men drowning or burning.

A great many of them were awarded the Purple Heart; some the Bronze or Silver Star, but then for many years, they tucked away their medals and their memories and did not reveal why or how they came by these awards, given to them by a grateful nation that remained—for many decades—blissfully unaware of their sacrifices.

CHAPTER ONE

'Over Here'

American Troops in England and their experiences

At 4 p.m. on Sunday 28 November 1943, Franklin D. Roosevelt was wheeled into the conference room of the Soviet Embassy in Tehran, where Joseph Stalin was waiting, a little impatiently. In a dark, pinstriped suit, his body erect and purposeful, Roosevelt soon began to appreciate the stern leader standing before him. Before long, they were joined by Winston Churchill, who arrived with his General Staff in tow. The weather, while not exactly tropical, was warmer than in England, where the damp, cold climate reflected the growing misery of the population, now facing its fourth Christmas at war. It was the first time the three great leaders had all attended a conference together and, although Roosevelt and Churchill had met on several previous occasions, the American and Russian leaders had never been in the same room before. There was an air of uncertainty, perhaps even distrust between the three men. This was born out of the fact that, while Roosevelt and Churchill had, until this point, been the more powerful leaders, Stalin was now in the ascendency. The Russians had defeated the German forces at Stalingrad, giving them—and their leader—the upper hand; Roosevelt's health was suffering under the mounting pressures of the war and Great Britain's power and influence were now in decline: indeed it would probably be fair to say that it was the 'beginning of the end' of her status in world leadership. Nonetheless, they had all come to Tehran to talk, and talk they must: some very important decisions needed to be made about the future direction of the war.

Over the ensuing four days, the three men and their advisors undertook a series of discussions around the table. Winston Churchill also presented Joseph Stalin with the Sword of Stalingrad, an accolade awarded by King George VI and the British people in recognition of the German surrender. Then, on the evening before the conference broke up, a birthday dinner was held for Mr Churchill at the British Legation, attended by both Marshal Stalin and President Roosevelt. Finally, the 'Big Three', as they became known, and their staffs and assistants went their separate ways, returning to their own nations to fight their respective wars, declaring: 'We came here with hope and determination. We leave here, friends in fact, in spirit and in purpose.'

Among the many items on the Agenda was the planning for Operation Overlord: the long-awaited invasion into Northern Europe. Stalin, keen to distract the German forces from the Russian Front had been pressing his Western Allies to launch a second front for a considerable time. He was not the only one who felt that a Second Front was essential. The British, in particular, believed that, while the Russian front needed protection from the German onslaught, it must also be maintained at all costs and had even considered sending both land and air forces to assist the Red Army should it become necessary. The greatest fear at the time was that, should the Russians be defeated, the Germans would be able to turn all of their attention and the might of their millions of soldiers to the Western Front, which Britain was ill-equipped to defend. Roosevelt and Churchill had already agreed on an invasion against the coast of Northern France at the Casablanca Conference during the previous January, although the question of who was to command the invasion had yet to be finalised. So, in Tehran, as the three men sat around the table, it was decided that this vital assault would take place during the late spring of 1944, probably in May. Stalin also consented to mounting an attack on the German border at roughly the same time, thus drawing some of Hitler's troops away from the Channel. As far as the Russian leader was concerned, he was satisfied with this plan, having finally got everyone to agree to a date for the planned attack and he was happy that the finer details could be arranged between his two allies.

Earlier in 1943, Roosevelt and Churchill had discussed who, out of the two countries, should take charge of the anticipated invasion. Churchill believed that it should fall under British command, due to their longer and greater experience in fighting against the German forces over the previous four years of the war. Roosevelt argued that, as the majority of the forces would be American, they would expect to be led by one of their own commanders and might take exception to being subordinate to British officers and commanders. The matter was debated for some time, with both men initially intransigent. However Churchill eventually came round to Roosevelt's way of thinking—he really had little choice in the matter—but the problem of who precisely would take charge remained unanswered for many months to come. In the meantime, however, plans had to be drawn up, so an interim Chief of Staff Supreme Allied Commander (COSSAC) was appointed, in the form of Lieutenant-General Sir Frederick Morgan, commander of British 1 Corps.

Morgan had been destined for the military from an early age and was a graduate of the Royal Military Academy, Woolwich. During the First World

War, he had served in the Artillery and was twice mentioned in dispatches. Then between the wars, Morgan had risen through the ranks, serving largely in India. In March 1943, he was tasked with drawing up the preliminary plans for the invasion and was expected to present his strategies by the beginning of July, knowing from the outset that his role was temporary and that he would be replaced by another commander-in-chief, prior to the actual attack itself. Although he did not realise that his replacement would almost certainly not be British, Morgan was quick to appoint Americans within his team, his deputy being Major General Ray Barker. A veteran of the First World War, having served in the 13th Field Artillery, Barker continued in this branch of the army after that conflict, eventually winning promotion to the rank of Brigadier General in July 1942, becoming the Deputy Chief of Staff, European Theatre in 1943 and then Deputy Chief of Staff at Supreme Headquarters Allied Expeditionary Force.

Morgan had immediately appreciated that the two nations must work together on all aspects of the planning and execution of the invasion, but despite his best efforts to maintain an *entente cordiale* between the American and British commanders on his team, there remained an inherent sense of distrust between the two sets of officers, which became more and more obvious as time progressed. This, coupled with differing perspectives on operational procedures, caused a great deal of friction which, in turn prevented almost every aspect of the invasion, from the minute to even the most important, being agreed upon. Morgan had hoped to at least gain a consensus as to destination, timing and operations, but this proved impossible. He realised—as he would later write—that 'at this time our army lay with its head in southern England and its tail in the neighbourhood of the western seaboard of the United States.' For the invasion, the British favoured the Pas de Calais, while the Americans preferred the beaches of Normandy, and there were even some officers, in both camps, who thought that mounting a cross-channel assault was untenable at that point in time. Morgan tried—and failed—to get all parties to reach some amicable arrangement and, eventually, it fell to Lord Louis Mountbatten, in his role as Chief of Combined Operations, to get everyone around the table to actually talk to each other calmly and properly until they could thrash out an agreement. So, in June 1943, the Americans won the day and it was decided that the invasion force would attack against the Normandy coast. This decision made, it then became necessary for the Americans to start amassing troops and equipment on the south coast of England in sufficient numbers to launch a successful assault.

Meanwhile, on the other side of the Atlantic, as early as the spring of 1942, the American Chiefs of Staff had already begun their own planning for the second front. Although at this stage, the precise timing and whereabouts of an invasion were very much undecided, the chiefs wanted to be sure that such an attack was practical and many of them, in common with some of their British counterparts and colleagues serving in England, doubted the wisdom of crossing the English Channel at all. Brigadier-General Dwight D. Eisenhower was serving on the General Staff in Washington DC, his role being to create war plans aimed at defeating Japan and Germany. He demonstrated how a cross-channel attack could be achieved by the employment of sufficient simultaneous supporting air and naval power, combined. He presented this plan to his superiors and it was passed up the chain of command having been approved by all parties, including the President and, when shown to Churchill and his Chiefs of Staff, it also met with their acceptance.

Eisenhower, a graduate of West Point, had served in the United States during the First World War, despite attempting many times to be transferred overseas. Between the wars, with the rank of major, Eisenhower served mainly as a commander of a tank battalion, working closely with George S. Patton, as well as working with General John Pershing at the American Battle Monuments Commission, where he produced a guide to the American battlefields in Europe. During the 1930s he served under several different generals in America before leaving with MacArthur for the Philippines, returning to Washington in 1939.

Despite the acceptance of Eisenhower's plan, his lack of military combat experience led to his initial dismissal as a potential commander for the advance into northern Europe and both the British and many Americans favoured General George C. Marshall, the US Army Chief of Staff, as the Supreme Commander of the Allied Forces. However, Eisenhower's success in leading Operation Torch, the British-American invasion of French North Africa in November 1942, changed the opinion of many involved in making this decision, making him a front-runner to lead the attack into mainland Europe. In his role as COSSAC, Morgan had gone to President Roosevelt and asked for 'your Army, your General Marshall, and your Ambassador Biddle,' to which the President replied that he could spare the Army, but that he did not feel that 'General Marshall could be spared.' He was simply too valuable serving as the Army Chief of Staff. Eisenhower was, therefore, finally appointed Supreme Commander in December 1943. The delay in making this late engagement gave him less than six months to complete the plans for the invasion, which was then anticipated as taking place at the end of May 1944. Eisenhower's first act was to briefly return to Washington, while sending his Chief of Staff, Major General Bedell Smith to join Field Marshal Montgomery, British Commander of the 21st Army Group in England to view the plans for Operation Overlord.

By the time of Eisenhower's appointment, his own strategy, coupled with the ones created by Morgan and his team, had ensured that there were already over one and a quarter million American soldiers stationed in various camps around the United Kingdom, awaiting their fate.

. . . . .

In the autumn of 1942, John Henry Hill, a married man with a young son, training in the United States Naval Reserve, was stationed at Marine Barracks, North River at Jacksonville in North Carolina. He, like his comrades, enjoyed nothing more than a little time off to relax and explore the local area, but found that most of the time, he was kept busy drilling and on the firing range. When he was off duty, he had discovered that—among the other attractions on the base—there was a café where the men could get a 'very good meal for 50 cents'.

Not long after his arrival at Marine Barracks, Hill had already begun to wonder at military organisation. For example, he marvelled at the amount of kit he had been issued, which consisted of a 'heavy overcoat, eighteen pairs of pants, 5 different suit coats, overcoat, one top coat, khaki ties and black and three caps, two summer and one winter'. He almost certainly had more clothes given to him by the quartermaster than he had in his entire wardrobe at home in Boston and wondered if he would ever 'be able to wear out, or wear half of these during the duration'.

The base covered over 200 square miles of ground, arranged in individual areas, each of which contained 'barracks, a church, a moving picture house, recreation hall and mess hall, all laid out in little streets', resembling small towns. Marine barracks had been constructed in 1941 on a site which contained over ten miles of beach, making it an ideal base for training troops in the art of amphibious landings.

Throughout his training, like many, Hill continually expected to be sent out to Japan to fight against those whom the Americans perceived as the real enemy but, as the months dragged on, he remained at the base in North Carolina, leaving only for training exercises in Maryland, where he was taught 'fire drills and abandon ship drills'.

As each new batch of marines came in for training, Hill's responsibility as a junior officer was to take care of all the supplies that arrived for these groups of men and to see that everything was despatched with them when they left to go overseas. He watched each group of men leave, wishing he could join them, instead of remaining behind. Time progressed and some of Hill's friends were sent to other camps as instructors—a fate which he dreaded: he wanted to see some action and was beginning to grow impatient.

Finally, in the autumn of 1943, Hill was moved, but still his ambition to fight was thwarted. He was not to be sent to Europe or Japan, but instead, he found himself at the US Naval Amphibious Training Base, Solomons Branch in Washington DC. He spent Thanksgiving on board ship, where a 'swell dinner' was served, reminding him of his grandmother's cooking. Hill anticipated that on 26th November, the crew would be assigned and that by the early part of the New Year, they would be on board their new ship, although their ultimate destination was, as he put it, 'anyone's guess'. As it turned out, Hill was quite correct, as the ship on which he was to serve, USS LST-531 was commissioned on 17 January 1944.

Having crossed the Atlantic, Hill arrived in Scotland at the end of March, but began his journey south the very next day, which he regretted. He found that the Scottish countryside reminded him of 'the hills of New Hampshire and Maine' and would have liked to spend longer there enjoying the scenery. Within a few days, Hill was settled in 'Southern England', although he was unable to tell his family exactly where he was stationed. What he did reveal was what he found, on going ashore. One of the towns, he said, was 'pretty well bombed', describing it as a 'shambles'. He was also surprised, he said, by the attitude of the British public, who moved along with their lives at a slow pace, seemingly unaware that there was even a war going on!

Other men were not so keen as John Hill to see action in Europe. Patsy Giacchi had been drafted at the age of eighteen, following the Japanese attack on Pearl Harbor. After just thirteen weeks of training at Camp Lee, Virginia, he was surprised to find that he was on board the Cunard liner *Mauritania*, bound for Liverpool in England, leaving behind his sweetheart, Emily. Once in England, Patsy began six months of intensive training in preparation for the D-Day landings.

Meanwhile, other officers found the training most useful and necessary, considering what they were about to face. Lieutenant Eugene Eckstam was a new naval reserve medical officer and had only just completed his senior year and internship. He felt 'totally unprepared for what was to follow' and believed that his training had been 'short'. His first task was to work at the Great Lakes Naval Training Station in Illinois where he examined an 'average of 1,700 recruits a day'. After this, he reported to Lido Beach, Long Island where a group of forty corpsmen and two physicians were formed into 'Foxy 29'—the codename for the medical unit assigned to LST-507, on which Eckstam was to serve. They left Lido Beach for England on 10 March 1944, where they continued their training at Fowey in Cornwall. Despite this, Eckstam still felt that he had 'little preparation for an invasion with major casualties'.

In Brooklyn, John Maltese had just graduated from high school and was looking forward to starting college and training to become an accountant. After a hard childhood, he hoped to better himself. However, in April 1943, he was drafted and sent to Camp Edwards in Massachusetts, where he began twelve weeks of basic training, which he describes as 'barbaric', explaining that the men were drilled with the motto 'kill or be killed' which ensured that they paid attention at all times. Once this initial training was complete, he was transferred to the 462nd Amphibious Truck Company, which was part of the 1st Engineering Special Brigade and sent to Fort Moultrie in South Carolina where he and his comrades practiced driving their DUKWs from ship to shore.

On 15 January 1944, Maltese was sent overseas, crossing the Atlantic and landing in Liverpool where they stayed in camps until they were moved and billeted in private homes with local people to make way for infantry men who were also arriving from America. Living among the locals gave Maltese and his friends, a different perspective of life in England.

· · · · ·

Almost all of the American soldiers and sailors found that life in England was very different to life at home in the United States. Many of the US servicemen who had already crossed the Atlantic in preparation for the invasion into Northern Europe, were stationed in the South West, in Dorset, Devon and Cornwall, where they discovered that rural England was rather a culture shock. England itself was different enough, but the West Country seemed like another world. In place of cars, they found horse-drawn carts, travelling along extremely narrow roads, lanes and tracks, bordered by long-established high hedgerows. These obliterated the views of the rolling countryside, but even when the American soldiers did manage to capture a glimpse of the fields and pastures, they found them to be tiny compared with those in their homeland. The buildings were made of 'cob—a mixture of granite, straw and clay—some houses had thatched roofs, and many of them had no indoor bathroom facilities or electricity. It was little wonder, therefore, that the Americans not only believed they had travelled to a different country, but also to a different century: one they might have, perhaps, read about in books but not one they ever expected to experience at first hand.

The Americans set up camps all over the South West of England where they trained their men, prepared and maintained their vehicles and got used to life in a foreign country. Their arrival had an enormous impact on the locals too, many of whom remember them with mixed feelings, as men who brought sweets, chewing gum and chocolate, which they gladly handed out to the children of the villages, but who were also brash and loud, compared to their quieter British counterparts. John Spooner was a local boy who lived in Teignmouth, Devon. Aged fourteen, his older brother and father were serving overseas and he was desperate to grow up quickly, so that he could join them.

One day, while out on his brother's bicycle, he came across an American jeep outside a public house in the village of Chudleigh. While investigating this strange vehicle, he was surprised to be offered a ride in it by two marines who appeared from the pub. He enjoyed the ride with them, but was enormously disappointed when they left him at their base at Heathfield and he had to make his own way back to the pub to collect his bicycle. Later that evening, in the window of the local post office, John noticed an advertisement for a general labourer to help out at the US base. John dashed home and asked his mother's permission and then telephoned to the base and spoke to a Sergeant McKinnon, who offered him the job. He started work the next Saturday, clearing up in one of the warehouses. He enjoyed the work and found most of the US servicemen only too glad to talk to a young lad, who seemed keen to help them out.

The US servicemen had been issued with a small handbook, entitled *A Short Guide to Great Britain*, which was produced by the War and Navy Departments in Washington DC. Within its pages, the soldiers read about how they were expected to behave, as well as finding explanations of the differences in language and etiquette. They were not surprised to read that Britain and its people might look 'shabby' to their eyes, but it was pointed out that this was only to be expected in a country that had been at war for several years, and that they would win no friends by pointing out the failings of their hosts. The handbook contained a great deal of advice, such as the fact that British 'reserve' should not be mistaken for rudeness; cricket is a 'slow game' when compared to baseball; that while the British could not make a 'good cup of coffee', neither could the Americans make a 'good cup of tea'—which they were advised was an 'even swap'. In one section of the handbook, they were reminded of the role of British women in the war. This applied not just to the British housewife, in her apron, who fed her children on scant rations, 'lived through high explosive air raids' and worried about her husband overseas, but also to the many women in uniform. These may be officers, the American soldiers were informed, and would expect to give orders to lower male ranks and have them obeyed, without question or comment. The female officers had earned this right and the American soldiers were informed that the sight of a ribbon on the tunic of one of these officers did not signify that she had knitted 'more socks than anyone else in Ipswich'. The men were given advice on the differences in currency, weights and measures as well as understanding the British accent. They were warned not to boast about earning more money than the British 'Tommies' they were fighting alongside and finally that they must NEVER, under any circumstances, criticise the King and Queen. The wise parting shot of the handbook stated:

It is always impolite to criticize your hosts;
It is militarily stupid to criticize your allies.

These American soldiers were not being corralled in the South West of England simply to await the invasion: training them was an essential part of the preparations for Operation Overlord. Many of the troops concerned had not been involved in any form of combat before, except for a minority, who had been in other theatres, such as the Sicilian campaign. They needed to understand what was expected of them in an amphibious landing; how to capture the German strongholds; establish and maintain beachheads and lines of supply that would endure enemy counter-attacks and keep the invading forces equipped and fed for many months as they advanced across occupied Europe. This meant not only training the men, but also the officers and commanders who would lead them into battle. In late 1943, a series of exercises was planned to take place in the early part of the following year, to enable everyone concerned to learn the necessary skills and gain the maximum experience possible, given the most important restrictions of not alerting the enemy to excessive activity and maintaining secrecy.

One of the first tasks at hand for those in command, was to find a suitable location on the south coast for conducting these exercises. The site concerned had to closely resemble the Normandy beaches where the landings would take place, but it was also necessary that the troops be able to use live ammunition to make the exercises as realistic as possible. After some deliberation, the site selected was Slapton Sands in the South Hams area. It was a reasonable distance from any of the genuine Operation Overlord installations, so if any activity was noticed by the enemy, it was hoped that the real intentions of the Allies would remain a secret. Additionally, the area itself was rural and was sparsely populated when compared with other nearby districts and, therefore, disturbance to the local population could be kept to a minimum. This latter aspect was of considerable concern, given that, due to the secrecy involved and the use of live ammunition, the entire population of several villages in the South Hams district would have to be completely evacuated.

CHAPTER TWO

'We'll Meet Again'

The evacuation of the South Hams

Lieutenant General Sir Hugh Jamieson Elles had a military background. He had served in the First World War, initially with the 4th Infantry Division, then with the 10th Infantry Brigade and was wounded during the Second Battle of Ypres in April 1915. By the autumn of 1916, he had been placed in charge of the Heavy Branch (the forerunner to the Tank Corps) and at the Battle of Cambrai in November 1917, Elles led 350 tanks across no man's land, causing mass panic among the German soldiers. Initially, this assault appeared to have brought about an early victory in the battle, but the Allied troops would later be driven back by a German counter-attack. At the end of the First World War, Elles took command of the Tank Corps Training Centre at Bovington in Dorset, before undertaking several War Office roles. Then, upon his retirement, he was appointed South West Regional Commissioner. This position meant that, in the event of an enemy invasion or occupation, Elles would have taken command of the South West area of England, in terms of resistance against the enemy.

As such, within this role, it fell to this experienced campaigner to call two meetings on Monday 8 November 1943 in the historic castle, set on the highest point above the city of Exeter. The first of these meetings was attended by local council representatives, members of the voluntary services and charities, such as the Women's Royal Voluntary Service (WRVS) and the Royal Society for the Prevention of Cruelty to Animals (RSPCA), as well as the Red Cross. At the second meeting, later in the day, Elles faced a number of clergymen from the South Hams district. His duty in each of these meetings was to inform those gathered before him that a mass evacuation was required, which would affect 30,000 acres of land incorporating the villages of Torcross, Stokenham, Chillington, Blackawton, East Allington, Slapton, Strete, Frogmore and Sherford as well as many smaller hamlets. This area included 180 farms, as well as many small businesses and shops, with the evacuation affecting some 750 families, amounting to approximately 3,000 civilians.

Those attending the meetings were familiar with the district and knew the South Hams area of Southern Devon to be a fairly typical rural part of England during the Second World War. Children played in the lanes and fields; the men worked the land, ran local shops and joined the home guard. Many were not required to enlist in the army because their occupation was deemed essential to the war effort, but those who did, had gone willingly to do their duty. Housewives tended their kitchen gardens, growing vegetables for their families; land girls helped out on the farms and the younger women of the villages either worked in the family businesses or in munitions factories in nearby towns. The war affected them, naturally, but not in the same way as those who inhabited the major towns and cities, who experienced the dangers of bombing raids, the harshness of rationing and the separation caused by the evacuation of their children.

By late 1943, Britain had been at war for over three years and some of the evacuees, who had been staying in rural areas, like the South Hams, had returned home, their cities deemed to now be safer to inhabit, the fear of bombing raids having receded. Generally the country communities in the South West of England, like many others across the land, had settled into a routine, if rather war-weary way of life.

The news of the evacuation had first been broken to the chairman of Devon County Council, Sir John Daw on 4th November via a telephone call from the War Cabinet, and one of the biggest problems faced by the local dignitaries, which was discussed during these initial planning meetings at Exeter Castle on 8th November, was the lack of notice they had been given. All people, possessions, machinery, animals and, where possible, usable crops, must be cleared from the area by 20th December. This meant there were just six weeks to complete a monumental task.

It was only fair that the civilians who inhabited the evacuation area should be informed as soon as possible of what lay in store, so meetings were hastily arranged by the end of that week. On Friday 12th November, a bitterly cold morning, the first of these meetings was convened at East Allington Church, towards the southern end of the village. In the chair was Hugh Fortescue, 5th Earl Fortescue, the Lord Lieutenant, who declared the meeting open at 11 a.m. The church was packed with locals, all keen to discover what was happening and why these meetings had been called so urgently and with so little notice. Earl Fortescue was greatly respected by everyone in the district. He, like Elles, had fought in the First World War, was twice wounded, mentioned in despatches and won the Military Cross in 1917. His only son Hugh, Viscount Ebrington, had died on 17 July 1942, fighting at El Alamein.

Although the public notices announcing the meetings had given a very broad outline of the evacuation, it fell to Earl Fortescue to pass on the news to the villagers and farmers that they must pack up their belongings and leave their homes for an indefinite period of probably not less than six months. At the meeting, Fortescue was joined and reinforced by representatives of the British government from the Ministries of Food and Power, Health, Labour and Transport, the US Military, the Royal Navy and the WRVS, all of whom fielded questions from the concerned and shocked locals. Further meetings were held that afternoon at Stokenham Church and the following day at Blackawton Church and Slapton Village Hall, these latter two being chaired by Sir John Daw. Everyone in the vicinity was encouraged to attend a meeting and employers were asked to give their employees time off, so as to ensure that everyone was present to hear the news and that no-one missed out on finding out the vital information that was required to make the evacuation run smoothly.

Even before the meetings, some of the locals had already heard rumours about military manoeuvres. Some had even heard surprisingly accurate whisperings of an evacuation, but these ideas were quickly put down as impossible: almost no-one believed that an entire district could be, or would need to be, evacuated. It is hardly surprising, therefore, that the reaction of the villagers to these announcements was one of great shock. Many thought that the physical task of moving that number of people, with all their possessions and livestock would prove unmanageable—especially within the allocated timeframe; others found it hard to believe that, at a time of national food shortages, the government would ask farmers to abandon their crops and fertile land. For some, especially the elderly, the prospect was a daunting one and a few people were extremely distraught. Some of the older villagers had never left their immediate vicinity or travelled in a car during their entire lives, so the idea of packing up all of their worldly possessions and moving many miles away to be among strangers was unsettling, to say the least. Despite these many doubts and fears, almost all of the local inhabitants accepted the news quite philosophically, resigning themselves to their fate and accepting that this was to be their contribution to the war effort.

The job of evacuation was monumental and required great organisation on the part of the authorities. An Information Notice was sent to every household within the evacuation area, explaining the procedures that would be employed and that must be followed. Information centres were set up at Stokenham and Blackawton, where individuals could go to ask their own, more personal, questions that could not be answered by the details provided in the Information Notice. Householders were advised to move as early as possible. While it was understandable that they would want to remain in their own homes for as long as they could, the authorities wished to avoid a last-minute rush for transport and removals assistance. The matter of compensation fell to the Admiralty, but the local MP, Colonel Ralph Rayner spoke out in the House of Commons, stating that the sacrifices being made by his constituents in having to "hand over their hearths and homes at the stark call of duty" should warrant generous recompense.

Villagers who were unable to find their own alternative accommodation with friends or relatives outside of the evacuation area, were told that they could be found somewhere to live by the local authorities, but they could be offered no guarantees as to where this would be and were told that in all probability they would be billeted in an already occupied property. People who agreed to take in villagers from the evacuation area were to be paid a billeting allowance.

In the early days of the evacuation, those people who owned their own vehicles were encouraged to use them to move furniture and belongings to their new accommodation and petrol coupons were made available at the information centres. However, once the Americans began to move into the area after the first couple of weeks, more restrictions were placed on the movement of vehicles and civilians had to make use of the transport provided by the authorities. For those who needed to store their furniture and belongings, the authorities were prepared to make arrangements for this.

The War Agricultural Executive Committee were on hand at Blackawton to advise farmers on the removal or disposal of livestock and crops, as well as to find work for agricultural workers, whose skills might be required on other farms outside of the evacuation area. These workers were told not to go seeking employment by themselves, as the War Agricultural Executive Committee knew where they were most needed and would place them appropriately. For others who needed to find employment, representatives from the Ministry of Labour were on hand at the information centres to offer advice.

Shopkeepers faced a different set of problems, as not only must they move their homes, their stocks and their belongings, but they also faced losing their livelihoods. In this instance, they were assisted by the Ministry of Food or the Board of Trade, who visited each shopkeeper in turn to offer guidance. Those who sold food and planned to leave the area prior to the final departure deadline, were told to advise the Food Executive Officer in Kingsbridge, so that alternative arrangements could be made, in order to keep that village or area supplied with the relevant foodstuffs until all the inhabits had left.

Children had to deal with the upheaval of changing schools, although many older students were able to remain at their existing secondary schools which were already situated in the larger towns outside of the evacuation area. All these students had to do was to amend their travel arrangements accordingly from their new, temporary homes. The same could not be said for the younger children and these changes meant that primary and junior schools outside of the area had to make room for all of the additional students who were now requiring space. At that time, all pensions were paid via the Post Office local to where people lived, so it was necessary to change the records of everyone who received a pension or other government assistance. Additionally, the Post Office had to arrange that all mail be redirected and civilians were reminded that they should notify their change of address to family members who were serving with the armed forces.

Churches in the area needed to be made safe, so experts were brought in to deal with the protection and preservation of all fixtures that could not be removed, most of which were old and valuable. Once this was completed, the Bishop of Exeter sent out a message to every parish, which was to be left on the door of each church within the evacuation area. It read:

To our Allies from the USA,

This church has stood here for several hundred years. Around it has grown a community, which have lived in these houses and tilled the fields ever since there was a church. This church, this churchyard in which their loved ones lie at rest, these homes, these fields are as dear to those who have left them as are the home and graves and fields which you, our allies, have left behind you. They hope to return one day, as you hope to return to yours, to find them waiting to welcome them home. They entrust them to your care meanwhile and pray that God's blessing rest upon us all.'

Although there was a general acceptance of the situation, there were those who really struggled to come to terms with what was happening and, out of this a few individual tragedies arose. One man committed suicide rather than leave his home; another woman had a heart attack and died during the process of packing her belongings; and an elderly couple managed to make the move, but within two weeks of leaving their home, both had fallen ill and passed away. Despite the public safety and military necessity for the evacuation, which everyone understood, it was still a very fearful time of private loss for everyone involved, from which some would never recover.

As in many such situations, everyone rallied around to help and, as the deadline approached, more and more Americans began to appear within the evacuation area. Rather than standing by and watching, they joined in, helping to move heavy furniture, loading vans and packing sandbags around priceless monuments and artefacts in the area's churches. Although it could be said that the Americans were ultimately responsible for the removal of the local inhabitants, the villagers understood that the G.I.'s themselves were not to blame and appreciated their kindness in doing whatever they could to lessen the blow of leaving their homes. The soldiers seemed to sympathise and understand how they would feel to be placed in the same position in their own properties back home.

As the weeks progressed, the villages and farms within the evacuation area became more and more deserted. The once busy roads and country lanes, bustling village shops and women chatting in the streets were soon a thing of the past. The fields were empty of livestock and the inns no longer rang out with the sounds of cheerful carousing at the end of a hard day's toil. There were no church services and finally, the last of the locals took their leave. As they did, the evacuation sentries moved into place and a strange silence descended. On 20th December, the electricity was cut off and all government assistance ceased. No further food supplies were granted into the area. Despite this, a very small number of families remained for a few extra days. These were generally people living in outlying farms who had been unable to move due to transportation difficulties, although there were other practical reasons for delay. The Trent family of Dittiscombe Farm, for example, were allowed to remain on their farm over Christmas in order to finish clearing their land of usable crops. It made no sense to waste good food supplies for the sake of a few extra days' work. It would have been a very austere Christmas indeed, given that there was no food to be had in the district, except that the American soldiers brought them some tinned goods and saved the day.

Before long, the hedgerows began to grow out of shape; gardens became overgrown with weeds and the cottages gathered dust. For those who had left, however, their experiences, which were many and varied, would remain with them.

Herbert Luscombe, a blacksmith from Stokenham, moved his equipment to nearby Beeson, where he shared the premises of the local smithy. However, with two men sharing the workload of one and less farmers in the area requiring their services, there was not so much for them to do. Herbert joined the Home Guard, which helped to fill his time, recalling that during the evacuation, he had often seen American troops driving around in an abandoned Baby Austin car.

The butcher's shop in Torcross was owned by the Hannaford family and they managed to find new accommodation at a farm at Chivelstone, renting a retail shop in Prawle. Despite this piece of good fortune, their business suffered due to the fact that most of their old customers, who had lived within the evacuation area, were now scattered far and wide. Additionally, they faced the problem that their new business premises had no electricity, so the storage of meat became very difficult.

Freda Luscombe and her family from Sloutts Farm were the last to leave Slapton. Freda moved to Muckwell Farm, the home of her fiancé, Tony Widger (the couple would marry in May 1944). One day, Tony made a secret visit back to Slapton and discovered that some of the buildings in the village had been damaged. Although he had not made it as far as Sloutts Farm, Tony returned to Freda after his excursion, wondering if she would ever be moving back to Slapton again. Meanwhile the rest of the Luscombe family moved to Littlehempston. However, there was not enough work for everybody, so Freda's younger brother Gordon, who was seventeen, tried to join the Navy. He was told that, instead, he must work for a farm contractor, driving a lorry containing fleeces to a woollen mill in Cornwall. Like Tony Widger, Gordon made a clandestine visit back to Slapton—or at least he almost did, but had the misfortune to be caught by the village policeman, who was there to prevent any looting. Gordon did manage to discover that the family farm was undamaged, before escaping back to Littlehempston.

The Bowles family moved from Slapton to Milton Farm in Dartmouth where Mr Bowles worked on the land. The two youngest boys attended school in the town and were able to observe the American troop movements and the build-up of ships in the harbour before the advance into Northern Europe. While none of them was keen to leave their home, they were helped by the American troops, who made them gifts of provisions and sweets for the children.

Builder, Godfrey Wills and his family lived in Strete and were the last people to leave the village. Having left so late, they were unable to find unfurnished accommodation, so their belongings were put into storage in Torquay, while they moved into Higher Farm in Beeson. Their living conditions were somewhat reduced: their table was a soap-box, with several smaller boxes used for chairs; their cooker was a primus stove and they slept on mattresses on the floor. Godfrey continued to do some building and repair work, as well as his duties in the Royal Observer Corps, based at Start Point.

The reactions of the local people varied from excitement to worries and fear. The children anticipated new schools and adventures, while their parents and elders were anxious about finding work and accommodation, storing their furniture and when they would be allowed to return to their homes. They were also concerned about the conditions they would face when they did manage to get back to their own villages and farms. Despite these fears, however, just about everyone accepted the situation. The country was at war and in wartime, people expected to make sacrifices.

CHAPTER THREE

'You'll Never Know'

The Build-up, Secrecy, Intelligence and Deception

When America entered the Second World War, following the Japanese attack on Pearl Harbor on 7 December 1941, her natural enemy became Japan, rather than Nazi Germany. As a result, there were many in the US who believed that all of their military efforts should, therefore, be directed in the Far East, rather than in Europe. It remained an uncomfortable truth, however, that at that stage, America lacked both the trained men and equipment needed to mount an effective campaign in the Pacific. Her attentions were, therefore, reluctantly diverted towards Europe, where she could join forces with the Allied nations and with Great Britain in particular. This left America very much, but very unwillingly, in the hands of the British as to where any initial attacks against Germany would take place. US Commanders pressed for an early assault across the English Channel, naming their fledgling plan Operation Sledgehammer. The Russians were also keen for this plan to be enacted as quickly as possible, so as to alleviate their own desperate situation on the Eastern Front. The British, however, wanted to focus attention in North Africa and the Mediterranean theatres, believing that it was premature to be considering a full-scale attack across the Channel at that time. Britain won the day on that occasion and, in the autumn of 1942 and into 1943, the Allies were occupied with Operation Torch (the invasion into French North-Africa) and the Sicilian Campaign, which was also known as Operation Husky.

In the meantime, the idea of a cross-Channel invasion was not forgotten, remaining at the forefront of the minds of the American Chiefs of Staff in Washington, so they continued with the build-up of US troops in Great Britain, under the codename of Operation Bolero. Although there was a steady influx of men, the main problem that faced the American planners at this stage was the shortage of landing craft, without which there was no point in even contemplating any kind of assault. While some of this shortage could be put down to a lack of production, even those ships that were available had been drafted in for use in the Mediterranean theatre, rather than being kept in reserve. Even though the American shipbuilders worked tirelessly building new craft, it took them four months to build a single LST (Landing Ship, Tank), so new and replacement vessels were slow in arriving. Additionally, the US shipyards were required to also build destroyers and escorts for use in the Atlantic to counter the U-boat threat, so could not dedicate themselves solely to the needs of the European theatre and the amphibious craft that were being requested to fulfil the potential requirements of any invasion that might be envisaged.

Even as the conflict was breaking out in Europe in 1939, the British government themselves had already realised the significance of landing craft in winning the war and had begun placing orders for vessels, such as Landing Ships Tank (LSTs) and Landing Crafts Tank (LCTs). The latter were built in Britain, but the former were constructed in America, where other more specialist vessels were also designed, including Landing Craft Vehicle/ Personnel (LCVP), Landing Craft Mechanised (LCM), Landing Craft Infantry (LCI) and the Landing Ship Dock (LSD). It then remained to train naval crews and army personnel how to man and land from these vessels. Despite this evident forward planning and the building capacity of both nations, it was uncertain, right up to D-Day, as to whether there would be sufficient numbers of these vital craft to actually mount the invasion.

As time progressed, though, ship-building continued and planning got underway, but the Americans grew more and more weary of Britain's reluctance to mount an early invasion into Northern Europe and began to openly discuss launching an attack on Japan instead. While this would almost certainly have been an impossible task to actually carry out, the initial discussions regarding a potential assault in the Far East had the desired effect of ensuring that the British focused on the more immediate need to look at appeasing her most important ally and crossing the Channel sooner rather than later, instead of placing all of her resources and attention on the Mediterranean front.

Once the decision had been made to concentrate on an attack into Northern Europe, both the Americans and the British saw the need for a rapid accumulation of US forces in the UK. However, they had rather different reasons for desiring this. Not surprisingly, America wanted to have a controlling majority of men, when it came to launching the invasion, giving them the right of leadership in the operation. The British commanders, on the other hand, harboured memories of the First World War and were reluctant to attack in Europe with a diminished force thus taking the risk of being overrun by the enemy. Despite the unhappy reminiscences of the First World War, however, the British also recalled that, while the Germans had appeared unbeatable in the spring of 1918, they had gone on to lose the war within eight months. British planners were keen to believe that history could be repeated.

After it had been decided that the cross-Channel invasion forces would strike against the coast of Normandy, it was prudent to disillusion the Germans as to the Allied intentions. In the summer of 1943, it fell to Lieutenant-General Morgan, in his continued role of acting-COSSAC, to plan and prepare diversions, lulling the Germans into believing that the attack might take place anywhere along the coast, other than Normandy. A series of operations was planned, beginning with Operation Starkey in September 1943. This was a fake invasion made by British and Canadian forces, supported by the Royal Navy, around Boulogne. The USAAF and RAF provided authentic bomber support in the hope of convincing the Germans that this was a legitimate invasion attempt. A secondary purpose of Operation Starkey was that it might well divert the much needed German forces from other theatres. In this aspect, it proved unsuccessful, at least in part due to the inability of the United States Army Air Force, the Royal Air Force and the Royal Navy, to fully commit to the operation, on account of other existing (and genuine) engagements. In another certain respect, Operation Starkey was a success, in that it suggested the Pas de Calais as the most probable target for the anticipated Allied invasion in the eyes of many German commanders.

Subsequent to Operation Starkey came Operation Wadham, which was launched at Brest with the aim of convincing the Germans that the Allies were committed to a two-pronged assault. This was an American operation, which failed from its very inception mainly due to the fact that a landing at Brest was outside of the range of Allied air support. Next came Operation Tindall, which was carried out by British and American forces based in Scotland, whose supposed aim was the capture of Stavanger in Norway. This operation was significantly more successful, in that its aim was to force the Germans to maintain their strength of twelve divisions in Norway, in case of an Allied invasion from that direction. This was achieved.

These early operations were not considered effective, their only redeeming feature being that they convinced the German High Command that the Allies had more men at their disposal than was really the case.

In 1944, further fake operations were undertaken, including Operation Fortitude, which had a Northern and Southern aspect to it. In the north, a fictional army was created in Edinburgh, its intent being to deceive the Germans into believing that an invasion of Norway was imminent. In the South, the 1st US Army Group was invented, its supposed objective being an invasion of the Northern French coast, specifically in the Pas de Calais region. Signals were intercepted showing that in both cases, Operation Fortitude had been a great success: the Germans did indeed believe that an invasion was highly likely and possibly imminent against either the Pas de Calais or Norway, or both.

There were several reasons why Operation Fortitude proved so much more successful than its predecessors. Firstly, the British made great use of double agents to feed false information to the German High Command; secondly, while some activity took place around the Normandy landing sites, it was ensured that this was kept to a minimum, so that in every practical sense, the focus appeared to be on the Pas de Calais. Finally, the fictitious 1st US Army Group had Lieutenant-General George S. Patton as its 'commander' and the employment of such a prominent officer convinced the Germans that the intent of this attacking force and the plans that went with it were entirely genuine. After all, it was assumed, the Allies would hardly waste such a well-respected general on a completely fake operation.

Despite the success of Operation Fortitude, Eisenhower, who was by now the Supreme Allied Commander of the Allied Expeditionary Force, faced the problems of controlling the external forces under his command, such as RAF Bomber Command and the US 9th Strategic Air Force. The commanders of these two units, Air Marshal Arthur Harris and General Carl Spaatz respectively, knew that they had significantly greater freedom if they operated outside of Eisenhower's control and they fought his every attempt to control their operations. Eventually, Eisenhower was able to gain overall command, but continued to find operational channels difficult to manoeuvre.

As part of the build-up to the invasion, the Allied Air forces launched Operation Pointblank, which formed part of the Combined Bomber Offensive, starting in June 1943 and running through 1944. The objective of this plan was to destroy German aircraft installations and factories, thus diminishing the value and ability of the Luftwaffe to respond on D-Day and afterwards. In addition, the bombers targeted petroleum, oil and lubrication plants, railways and other transport links, thereby totally disrupting the German lines of communication and supply, as well as making the movement of vehicles and men more difficult in the build-up to the invasion. During these operations, the Royal Navy made a request that the Combined Bomber Offensive might also turn its attention to the E-boat pens situated along the French coast. The naval commanders saw the German E-boats as a serious threat, but the Combined Bomber Offensive refused to mount any bombing raids against them until after Operation Overlord had already got underway. Harris and Spaatz had sound reasons for this refusal: the E-boat pens were heavily fortified, and it was doubtful whether a bombing campaign would have met with any degree of success. In addition, both commanders considered such raids to be a waste of men and resources, as they were likely to result in considerable loss of life and machinery for very little return.

General Eisenhower faced other difficulties that had to be overcome. Although Lieutenant-General Morgan's invasion plan was sound; Eisenhower, together with his ground force commanders, Generals Montgomery, Bradley and Dempsey, felt that Morgan's three-pronged attack was insufficient to land enough men and drive the Germans back into France. To the three existing beaches, codenamed Omaha, Gold and Juno, Eisenhower decided to add another two, named Utah and Sword, essentially creating two landings sites for the American Forces (Omaha and Utah), two for the British (Sword and Gold) and one for the Canadians (Juno). The addition of these two new landing sites made the shortage of landing craft an even more acute problem, especially as vessels were also now being used in US operations in the Pacific theatre.

Another difficult decision which had already been faced by Eisenhower was who to appoint as his immediate subordinates. Just as Morgan had decided on an American deputy, Eisenhower chose to appoint British commanders in all cases. In overall command of land forces, Eisenhower appointed General Bernard Montgomery. A veteran of the First World War, Montgomery had commanded the Eighth Army in the Western Desert and Sicily. The victory at the Battle of El Alamein, under his command, is often seen as a turning point in the war. Air Chief Marshal Sir Trafford Leigh-Mallory was given command of the air forces. Leigh-Mallory had served in the Royal Flying Corps during the First World War, rising to the rank of squadron commander. By the beginning of the Second World War, he was Air Officer Commanding of No. 12 (Fighter) Group before taking over command of No. 11 (Fighter) Group after the Battle of Britain. In 1942 he became the Commander-in-Chief of Fighter Command. Finally, command of the naval sections was given to Rear-Admiral Sir Bertram Ramsay, who was another First World War veteran, having served as part of the Dover Patrol off the Belgian coast. Although he had retired from the Royal Navy in 1938, Winston Churchill persuaded him out of retirement and he participated in many important naval operations, from the evacuation of Dunkirk to Operation Neptune (the landing operations element of Operation Overlord). All three of these officers were experienced men in their own fields with a track-record to prove it. Despite this, the senior American officers believed that they should have control of their own troops on the ground, so Eisenhower divided the assault troops into East, incorporating British and Canadian forces; and West, comprising the American troops. Eisenhower made it clear that Montgomery was still in overall command, but appointed secondary commanders for each section. General Miles Dempsey and General Harry Crerar were placed in charge of the British and Canadian Forces on the ground, respectively. Having been part of the rear-guard at Dunkirk, Dempsey then went on to help plan the invasion of Sicily and later led the invasion of Italy across the Strait of Messina. In January 1944, Montgomery appointed him commander of the 2nd Army. Crerar, a native of Ontario, served as an

Artillery officer in the First World War, before rising through the ranks in the General Staff during the Second World War. For the American forces in the West, the command was given to General Omar Bradley, a veteran of West Point, who had served under Eisenhower in North Africa, before replacing Patton as commander of II Corps.

Within the Naval forces, just as with Montgomery, Ramsay would retain overall command, but the US Western Task Force was led by Rear-Admiral Alan Kirk. A former naval attaché, Kirk had been an amphibious commander in the Mediterranean theatre between 1942 and 1943, taking part in landings at Sicily and Italy. The British Forces in the Eastern Naval Task Force were commanded by Rear-Admiral Philip Vian who, following his service in the First World War, had spent most of the inter-war years in the Mediterranean. During the Second World War, he participated in several pivotal actions, including the sinking of the Bismarck, Operation Gauntlet and the Malta Convoys.

Beneath Kirk, Rear-Admiral John Hall Jr had already been given command of the naval forces due to land at Omaha Beach but, once Eisenhower added the Utah landing site, a second commander was required. The US Chief of Naval Operations, Admiral Ernest J. King appointed Rear-Admiral Don P. Moon to this task. Hall, in charge of naval operations at Omaha, was responsible for the transportation of V Corps, under the command of Major-General Leonard Gerow. The Utah naval forces, under Moon's control, would convey VII Corps to their destination, led by Major-General Joseph Lawton Collins.

While the US Navy was to provide its own vessels for its sector of operations, it depended on Royal Navy port facilities. Rear-Admiral Kirk worked closely with Royal Navy Vice-Admiral Charles Little in Portsmouth and Rear-Admiral Sir Ralph Leatham in Plymouth.

Once all of these commanders had been appointed and a sufficient number of troops had been amassed in the south of England, the next step in the build-up to Operation Overlord, was training. The British carried out their exercises mainly off the coast of Hampshire and Sussex, while the Americans were based in the West Country: in Dorset, Devon and Cornwall. Most of the participating servicemen (and some of their commanders) had little or no experience of an amphibious landing, although some had taken part in Operation Torch or the landings at Sicily. As such, the training aspect of Operation Overlord was absolutely vital to its smooth running and ultimate success.

Before the Japanese attack on Pearl Harbor, only the US Marine Corps had received any training in amphibious landing techniques. However, afterwards, it became clear that if the Americans were going to operate in more than one theatre, the US Army would also need to be involved in the amphibious element of an attack. It was decided that, essentially, the Marines would focus their attentions on the Pacific theatre, while the Army would be based in Europe, although some joint operations were carried out.

With Slapton Sands and its surrounding area having already been evacuated in preparation and with the American troops being corralled in this region of England, this was where a lot of the US pre-invasion amphibious landing assault exercises took place—most especially the larger ones. Military intelligence informed the Allies that, while the German High Command still believed that the cross-Channel assault would land in the Pas de Calais region, Field-Marshal Erwin Rommel had also decided that the Normandy coastline needed reinforcing against a possible Allied attack. Rommel, a decorated First World War veteran, was a much respected leader and his suggestions were not ignored. As part of these defensive reinforcements, Rommel had decided to flood the lowlands behind the Normandy beaches to make an Allied advance more difficult. This geographical aspect was, fortunately, replicated by the Ley at Slapton, thus giving the Devon practice site another similarity with the real landing site.

As part of the planning for the training exercises, a team of commandos was sent across the Channel to the Normandy beaches to ascertain the composition of the sand and shingle, to see if it was suitable for landing heavy vehicles.

The United States Army and Navy men had only received rudimentary training in America before setting sail for Europe and, once in England, they had to learn quickly how to handle their craft and how to embark and disembark. Due to the shortage of landing craft, it became necessary to plan to load even more men and equipment onto each vessel than normal and this issue was one of the reasons for ultimately postponing the D-Day landings from the end of May to the beginning of June and also for the cancellation of Operation Anvil—a planned simultaneous assault in the Mediterranean, which was eventually carried out in August 1944 under the codename Operation Dragoon.

Training for US Troops began at the Assault Training Centre at Woolacombe in North Devon, where they were taught and practised new tactics of amphibious landings, prior to participating in the training exercises themselves. This centre was devised due to the fact that many of the American troops who were arriving in Britain had received no prior training in amphibious landings. The man who was given the task of setting up the centre was Lieutenant-Colonel Paul W. Thompson, who had arrived in England in January 1943 where he decided to gather together a team of experts and station them at Woolacombe and Braunton beaches, which bore a strong resemblance to the coastline of Normandy.

The first US troops to be trained there arrived on 1 September 1943 for a course which lasted three weeks and, over the next seven months almost 45,000 American soldiers passed through the centre. As part of their training, the troops would embark on landing craft from Braunton Burrows and participate in landings at Woolacombe Sands, sometimes using live ammunition, whereupon they would establish beachheads and then fight their way inland.

While this area of Devon was used for training the troops, Slapton Sands, in the south, was to be employed in the training of officers whose responsibility was to direct and control the units who had already completed their instruction while at Woolacombe.

The training exercises at Slapton Sands for Operation Overlord began in January 1944, with Operation Duck I, held to instruct elements of General Bradley's 1st Army in battalion and regimental sized landings. This involved troops from several units working together, managing and training on combined assaults and supply problems. Duck I was possibly the most important of the early major exercises, since it demonstrated several issues and problems which would have to be corrected for future exercises and for the Normandy landings themselves.

Duck I was divided into two phases. In the first, the troops were processed and embarked onto their respective landing craft. The second phase dealt with the assault itself. The men involved in this first exercise came from the 29th Infantry Division, the 175th Regimental Landing Team, and units of the 1st Engineer Special Brigade. There were also various attachments of the IX Air Force beach party and a Headquarters Group of V Corps.

Essentially, the exercise went according to plan, with the landings being successfully mounted but, following a debrief shortly afterwards, many criticisms were made, including:

- a lack of coordination between naval and army sections;
- the LST commanders' failure to understand the significance of landing their craft in exactly the right place;
- the planning of the whole exercise was generally too hurried and a suggestion was made that the planning group should be better coordinated and centrally located;
- the men took too long to disembark from the landing craft during the assault phase and it was agreed that, in a real battle, troops would have been killed by enemy gunfire;
- there were some vehicles that landed on the beach unloaded, while others were burdened down with too much equipment;
- the communications equipment was poor;
- there were security issues—radio silence was not maintained and the

camouflage employed at the assembly sites was insufficient.

While none of these problems, in isolation, is too shocking, when taken together, they are potentially catastrophic. Lessons had to be learned quickly because almost as soon as Duck I was completed, plans got under way for Duck II, which took place in late February and early March 1944. The units that had not been employed in the first exercise participated in this one, and it was deemed to have run more smoothly than its predecessor, although several issues still needed to be addressed.

Exercise Fox followed in the middle of March, taking the form of a full scale rehearsal for the landing at Omaha beach. The landing craft convoy to Slapton Sands was escorted by five Royal Navy destroyers and the RAF and 9th US Army Air Force also participated. As with both Duck exercises, several problems arose which would need to be addressed before D-Day. These included:

- a lack of coordination between the navy and the army as well as between different HQs;
- a lack of time between planning and assault;
- poor security, including insufficient camouflage and inadequate warnings of air raids;
- the unloading of the beach group was poor and there was a lack of coordination between the beach-masters and the coasters, resulting in troops being allowed ashore in the wrong order and delays in unloading equipment.

The troops used in both the Duck and Fox exercises were almost exclusively those who were destined to participate in the landings on Omaha beach. The 4th Infantry Division, which was due to attack at Utah beach, took part in smaller exercises which started on 13th March. These were codenamed Muskrat I and II, Otter I and II, Mink I and II, Beacher, Excelsior I–VI, Crimson I and II, Hawk I and II, Curveball I and II and Boomerang. Additionally, there were exercises covering marshalling, loading, medical and signals, all held between February and May.

These smaller exercises and the issues they raised and—in some cases— solved, all built up to the 'dress rehearsal' phase, which began at the end of April, with Exercise Tiger.

CHAPTER FOUR

'Counting the Days'

Planning for Exercise Tiger

The early exercises in the build-up to D-Day had highlighted several important issues and problems, one of the most significant of which was a lack of good, sound communications. This applied not only to American and British communications, but also to those between the United States Navy and Army forces. Despite the many exercises undertaken, this would remain a difficulty and it became imperative that, along with the other flaws singled out during the preparations, this aspect should be rectified during the later stages of training.

In addition, however, there were other problems and inter-departmental difficulties which fell under the broad heading of "communications", that also needed to be addressed. Some of these related only to the exercises themselves, rather than to Operation Overlord itself, but any inability to resolve problems at this stage would only cause difficulties, possible ill-will and perhaps, potentially critical delays later on. Eisenhower was faced with the need to settle any differences amicably, and while he did his best to gloss over the cracks that occasionally appeared he confronted an uphill battle most of the way.

One of the biggest hurdles in planning the final 'dress rehearsal' phase of the exercises was their close proximity to the Normandy landings themselves. Everyone responsible in the organising of the exercises was well aware of the fact that they were just that: they were practice runs and each individual involved in these preparations also all knew that their main focus needed to be on the main event that was still to follow. To have these training runs so close to the 'real thing' was deemed by many to be an unnecessary distraction and by some to be a monumental waste of time and resources. Many of the personnel involved in planning these final exercises were also pre-occupied with planning the D-Day landings themselves and some of the senior officers voiced their concerns that to divert too much attention away from the real operation might ultimately prove counter-productive and costly. Nevertheless, almost everyone concerned still needed training—not least the officers involved, and it was for them, as much as their men, that these final exercises were being planned.

The final two rehearsal exercises were codenamed Fabius and Tiger. Exercise Fabius was to involve all of the forces—British, American and Canadian—who would land at Gold, Sword, Omaha and Juno beaches during the Normandy invasion. Exercise Tiger was created purely for the officers and men whose destination during Operation Overlord would be Utah Beach.

The initial planning for Exercise Tiger took place in early February 1944, when the date was set for 22–30 April. Definite instructions were issued on the 1st of April, at which point VII Corps, who were directing the exercise, began preparations. All three regimental landing teams of the 4th Infantry Division were to be involved, together with the 1st Engineer Special Brigade, who would be in support. Airborne operations were to be supplied by 101st and 82nd Airborne Divisions.

The whole exercise was due to last nine days, with six being taken up by mounting and embarkation, which was to take place at Plymouth and Dartmouth/Brixham, involving some 25,000 men and 2,750 vehicles. It was agreed that the Royal Navy was to provide bombardment and escorts for the convoys.

It was vital that the two US commanders in charge of the exercise should manage to overcome the previously highlighted issues surrounding poor communications between the Army and the Navy. The commander of VII Corps was General Joseph Lawton Collins, a First World War veteran who had seen commands in Hawaii and Guadalcanal. His opposite number in charge of the naval forces for Exercise Tiger and, therefore, the Utah landings, was Rear-Admiral Don P. Moon. In terms of Operation Overlord, it was Moon's job to get Collins's troops and all their support materials from England to their destination on the north coast of France and disembark them safely. Moon had graduated from the United States Naval Academy in 1916 and served on several battleships before becoming commanding officer of the destroyer John D. Ford in 1934. By 1940 he was in command of a destroyer division, taking part in the invasion of North Africa in 1942. He was promoted to the rank of Rear-Admiral in 1944. Moon had no experience of an amphibious landing and Exercise Tiger was his first training operation, but this was not seen as an obstacle in his appointment to commander of Force "U".

When Collins first met Moon, the two got along quite well, but as they began to work together more closely, during the build-up to Exercise Tiger and, ultimately, the D-Day landings, Collins discovered that Moon was a very anxious character, who found it difficult to delegate responsibility to his junior officers. While this might be perceived as diligence, Collins—who continued to like Moon as a person—began to worry that Moon might be unduly prudent [or cautious] in his decisions and lacking in the necessary trust which a commander ought to have in his junior officers, especially when it came to the stresses of combat situations. None of this uneasiness between the two commanders augured well for the relationship they needed to forge, especially as one of the most important aspects of Exercise Tiger was to train the officers involved in their roles for the D-Day landings.

Being as Exercise Tiger was being seen as the first—and only—full 'dress rehearsal' for the Utah beach landings, it was decided that everything must be made as realistic as possible. The embarkation of the troops and equipment would begin on 22nd April, with 'D-Day' planned for the 27th at 07.30 (H-Hour). The ships containing the men and equipment would take a circuitous route from their embarkation points, rendezvous and then continue to Slapton Sands in order to replicate the amount of time they would spend at sea during the Channel crossing. This element gave cause for concern to Rear-Admiral Alan Kirk. In his role as commander of the Western Naval Task Force, he was acutely aware of the dangers of carrying out exercises so close to the enemy. Not only were there inherent security risks, in terms of the Germans potentially discovering the plans for Operation Overlord, but the Germans had laid mines in the Channel, the positions of which were unknown to the Allies. For Kirk, however, the most pressing danger was that posed by the presence of the powerful German E-boats, which were stationed at Cherbourg. Capable of speeds of around forty knots, the E-boats were able to make their attack and flee the scene before the Allied shipping even had the opportunity to react. So, while everyone was aware that Exercise Tiger was only a rehearsal and that it was only a part of the build-up to the Normandy Landings, it was also made very clear that the enemy threat was very real indeed and this information was reiterated several times during the preparations, by Rear-Admiral Moon to his captains on 25th April as well as by Rear-Admiral Kirk to all of the planners involved in both Exercises Tiger and Fabius and by Rear-Admiral Hall, commander of Force "O", who was preparing separately for Exercise Fabius.

Exercise Tiger itself was planned in two phases: firstly there would be the main assault on the beach. This would consist of the first infantry waves, landing during 27th April under heavy supporting fire from both air and sea. Following behind, in the second phase would be the reinforcements, in the form of the men and equipment required to consolidate the beachhead and press on inland, as well as maintain vital supply lines to the advancing troops. The men in this second wave included engineers, quartermasters, drivers and men from the Graves Registration and Chemical Decontamination Units, among others. Their tasks were to come onto the beach and inland behind the main infantry force, providing logistical and practical reinforcement. They also brought with them many vehicles, ranging from jeeps to trucks and tanks, as well as fuel and all the necessary supplies. Also included in this second wave were ten officers who, on D-Day would be carrying the plans for the Normandy invasion. These officers had been given the status of BIGOT, meaning that they were permitted to see and handle papers of a most secret nature. On D-Day itself, these men would be a part of the invading force and, therefore, they too needed to practice their roles in Exercise Tiger. Although they were not to carry the actual plans for D-Day with them during the exercise, they still had the knowledge of 'how', 'when' and 'where' the real events were to take place, making them very valuable passengers.

Over 300 ships were to participate in the exercise, ranging from the smallest landing craft, used for personnel, to the LSTs which carried the bulk of the equipment and reinforcements. The plan was that these enormous ships would arrive several hours after the assault troops, once the landing sites had been cleared of enemy defenders and would 'beach' themselves on shore, allowing the vehicles and men on board to be disembarked. They then had to wait until the tide came in before being able to depart. As well as the assault vessels and landing craft, there were also several ships stationed in Lyme Bay, situated to protect the convoys from any potential enemy attacks.

Rear-Admiral Leatham at Plymouth had already agreed that all shipping (whether American or British) would come under US Navy jurisdiction throughout both Exercises Tiger and Fabius, since this sector fell under the Western Naval Task force, under Rear-Admiral Kirk's overall command. Leatham further agreed that he would treat the US commanders as being in charge of the entire operation. This agreement led to problems in itself, however. For example, Leatham had consented that he would pass on to US naval chiefs any information he received regarding enemy activities during the exercises and also that he would suggest what, if any, action the American commanders should take. His reason for this latter comment was that the Royal Navy and RAF were providing support and radar cover and British forces had a better knowledge and understanding of the British coastal waters in which the exercises were taking place. As such, it could be said that it was hardly surprising that Leatham might suggest action, but the American commanders were affronted by his comment, taking it as a personal insult against their abilities to manage a given situation.

On land, the beach at Slapton Sands had been defensively 'dressed' to resemble the Normandy beach codenamed "Utah" and, rather than just practising the act of disembarking the troops and equipment, American soldiers were to be placed on shore to act as the 'enemy', their task being to defend the beach from the invading forces.

To make everything even more realistic, troops were given the same rations as they would carry on D-Day itself, which included two days' supply of water. Additionally, there would be simulated 'casualties' to allow the medics to train. 'Deaths' and 'burials' would take place in previously designated 'cemeteries' so that the Graves Registration Unit could undergo a rehearsal for the real event. There was also a provision for taking 'enemy' prisoners of war. Finally, orders were issued that live ammunition should be used. This not only applied to the soldiers, but also to the naval bombardment that would precede the 'invasion'. While this may have been deemed advantageous or even necessary to harden the troops and heighten the perceived danger and realism of the exercise, there were limits to the usefulness of this action. It was not intended that the advancing soldiers should actually come under live fire, or that they should advance into a hail of bullets. The naval bombardment was planned and timed so that the beach would be empty when it was carried out and the 'enemy' fire was to have strict restrictions as to how, when and where it was aimed. As such, the usefulness of live ammunition was surely limited. The Germans were not going to aim above the heads of the advancing soldiers; the naval bombardment was not going to wait for the beach to be empty. The 'realism' was staged. While it was hoped to give the soldiers a genuine idea of what would be involved on D-Day, this dangerous and, ultimately costly course of action was possibly taking things too far. Realism is one thing, but it was, perhaps, being carried to unnecessary extremes, as would be seen in the overture of Exercise Tiger.

The plan was that the 101st Airborne division would land four hours before H-Hour (H-4) behind the beach itself. However, there were insufficient planes available to mount proper airborne troop landings, so it was decided that the troops would be dropped in the Slapton Sands area by truck and would meet up, at their designated rendezvous point, with the advancing infantry.

It was believed that the first wave of troops required heavy support from both sea and air, but that the second wave of reinforcements did not need such back-up, as the 'enemy' (both during the exercise and in the actual landings) would already be pre-occupied in fighting the troops who had landed in the first wave and would not have time to worry about the forces who arrived in the second wave. As such, there was deemed to be less need for naval strength or back-up after the first day of the exercise.

As a result of the lessons learned in the earlier exercises, it was planned that balloons would be flown over Brixham and Torbay prior to and during embarkation to prevent enemy aircraft observing and bombing the area.

Final orders for Exercise Tiger were issued on 18th April, but even these were subject to last-minute changes, as between 21st and 24th April—while the embarkations were already under way—additional briefings were still taking place at the Royal Marine Barracks in Plymouth.

The follow-up convoy that would bring in the reinforcements after the initial landings had the codename of T-4 and its commodore was Commander Bernard Joseph Skahill. His convoy was due to sail on 27th April, after the troops in the first assault wave had already landed at Slapton Sands. However, as the day approached, Skahill became more and more alarmed that he had not received full orders from Rear-Admiral Moon and that no arrangements had been made for proper communications between T-4 and their Royal Navy escort. Both he and his communications officer, Lieutenant Moses Hallett raised this issue with Rear Admiral Moon's staff, but were told to refer to their operations orders, which they also had not received.

Following the final briefings at Plymouth on 24th April, Rear Admiral Kirk's staff boarded the Command Ship USS *Augusta* at Plymouth, followed by Kirk himself, the next day. From the *Augusta*, the landing exercise would be observed and reported upon. To these observers fell the task of ironing out any last minute problems that might hamper the 'real' landings at Utah Beach, which were now just over a month away. Rear-Admiral Moon went on board the Utah Force command ship USS *Bayfield* on the 25th of April and on the following day, the first troop ships of Exercise Tiger set sail for Slapton Sands.

CHAPTER FIVE

'Now is the Hour'

The Exercise Tiger Tragedy

It was 17.40 on 26 April 1944 when the USS *Bayfield*, the Force 'U' flagship, left Plymouth Sound to serve as Naval Headquarters during Exercise Tiger, overseeing and observing operations. The main assault landings were set to begin at 07.30 the following morning (H-Hour). At 03.30, paratroopers from the 101st Airborne Division were 'dropped' by truck behind the beach in a simulated jump, due to insufficient aircraft being made available for this exercise. Obviously, this simulation meant that their 'landing' was safe and uneventful and they immediately headed out towards their primary objectives, before meeting up with the assault troops, due to land on the beach in a few hours' time.

As the first stage of this assault process, the boats began to be lowered from the USS *Bayfield* at 04.15 and within two hours, General Collins and his staff had been put ashore, prior to the first wave of troops, to command, manage and observe the whole process from the Army's perspective. However, just before 06.30, the first tangible problem of the exercise arose. The commander of one element of the attacking forces (Green Assault Group) contacted Rear-Admiral Moon aboard USS *Bayfield* and informed him that some of the landing craft were running behind their allotted schedule. Moon had to decide quickly what he should do. If he was going to delay H-Hour, the decision must be taken immediately as the Royal Navy bombardment of the beach was about to begin—sixty minutes prior to the first troops landing. Ideally, he would have preferred to consult with General Collins, but the General was already ashore and could not be contacted by Moon. At 06.25, Moon made the decision: H-Hour would be delayed by one hour, until 08.30. Unfortunately, the communication issues, which had plagued the other exercises from the outset, continued to be a problem and some of the attacking troops did not receive the revised orders. They, therefore, began their landings on the beach at the previously allotted time of 07.30, just as the Royal Navy was beginning its bombardment of the shoreline with live ammunition to coincide with the new H-Hour of 08.30. Needless to say, there were some casualties, although precisely how many has never been made clear.

The remainder of the landing forces arrived at 08.30 and at this stage of the exercise, there occurred a second significant event, which if true, remains one of the most notable cover-ups of the whole operation. In a Barnes Review article of 1998, there is an account of investigations carried out by Christy Campbell and Nigel Lewis. In this report, we can see that Jim Cary, who was serving with the Royal Engineers, recalled seeing US soldiers jumping out of their landing craft and moving up the beach, where they came under fire from the 'enemy' troops, who had been stationed there to defend the position. However, Cary states that, rather than firing over the heads of the advancing men, the defenders fired directly at them and the attackers fell, wounded and dead, to the ground. On board LST-507, medical officer, Eugene Eckstam was aware, as the ship left Brixham, that 'there'd been casualties at Slapton', although whether these were as a result of the mis-timed bombardment or the 'friendly-fire' incident, is not altogether really clear.

Rumours persisted from then on of multiple deaths—with some claiming that these were well into the hundreds—and mass burials in unmarked graves. There had also been casualties during Exercise Duck I (caused by drowning), which were officially admitted after the war, but the 'friendly fire' incident at Slapton Sands has always been denied and even where it has been hinted at, the number of casualties remains unknown, but is thought to be nearer to one hundred than the 'several hundred' to which some have alluded.

It does seem hard to believe that men would fire live ammunition directly at their comrades rather than above their heads and, upon seeing the carnage that they were causing, that they would not cease firing. Some have argued that they might not have known that they were using live ammunition, but others have stated this to be impossible, saying that a soldier always knows what type of ammunition he has loaded into his weapon. However, these men were not 'soldiers' in the conventional sense. They wore a uniform and carried a gun, but for some of them, six months earlier, they had still been civilians, so one has to question whether they would have known, instinctively, what type of ammunition they were using. Whether or not this incident happened exactly as described and whether there were hundreds of deaths and mass graves might never be known, but it remains another enigmatic element of the Exercise Tiger story. In trying to analyse these two episodes of the casualties caused by the naval bombardment and the potential, but unproved 'friendly fire' incident, we must also remember that the widely respected Allied Naval Commander, Rear-Admiral Ramsay, after observing this debacle would comment in his diary: 'It was a flop and putting it off was a fatal error', suggesting that the delay of H-Hour was a significant and costly factor in all that went wrong that morning, but that he makes no mention of anything else going wrong.

Even once the main forces had begun to move ashore, unheeded, all did not go according to plan. There were delays in moving the men inland, so the beach soon became clogged with troops and equipment which, in reality, would have proved costly. Eventually, the beach was 'secured' at 15.30, but in his diary for that day, Ramsay would also comment: '… there was much to criticise, but the main thing was the lack of senior naval and army officers on the beach'.

Meanwhile, at 09.50 while the troops were landing at Slapton Sands, five LSTs assembled off Plymouth Sound and set off on their route towards Lyme Bay. LSTs are designated numbers, rather than names and these five sailed in the following order: 515 (the command ship), 496, 511, 531, 58 (towing two pontoon causeways). At 11.00, the five LSTs were joined by two escort vessels, HMS *Azalea* (a flower-class corvette) and HMS *Scimitar* (a First World War S-Class destroyer). However, almost immediately the *Scimitar* was ordered to return to Plymouth. She had been damaged the previous day in a collision with another LST and this damage, it was decided, required inspection. When the *Scimitar* arrived at Plymouth, the duty officer believed she had been sent back under the orders and, certainly with the knowledge, of Rear-Admiral Moon—after all, Exercise Tiger was a US-led operation, so this seems to be a fair assumption. He also seems to have believed that a new vessel had already been assigned to escort convoy T-4, so he took no further action.

At 19.00 these first five LSTs and their escort of one remaining Royal Navy corvette—HMS *Azalea*—sailed past Brixham, where they were joined by three further LSTs, numbers 499, 289 and 507, sailing in that order. The whole convoy then proceeded at approximately five knots in a circuitous route towards Slapton Sands.

It was not until 19.30—several hours after her arrival in Plymouth—that anyone there realised that no other vessel had been designated to replace HMS *Scimitar*. Lieutenant Shee, the commanding officer of the *Scimitar* was summoned and revealed that his orders had not come from Rear-Admiral Moon at all. Now the task remained to sort out what had happened and, more importantly, work out what to do about it.

In the meantime, as the convoy headed east, in the early hours of 28 April, at 00.20, the first of several flares were seen. There was no radar contact with any vessels noted by any of the LSTs, so no action was taken and no-one seemed to know the origin of the flares. HMS *Onslow*, an O-Class destroyer, was patrolling off Portland Bill and she reported sighting an E-boat, but it slipped

Mrs Cantrell:

Here is a schedule of the L.S.T. that our son was on as sent us by his captain. We think your son's ship would have been on this same schedule, as our boy told us that both ships had been side by side all the way.

Dec. 27, 1943   Picked up L.S.T. at Evansville, Indiana.

Jan. 2   1944   Departed Evansville for New Orleans.

Jan. 8   ""   Arrived New Orleans, for commissioning and fitting.

Jan. 25   ""   Departed New Orleans, for Panama City, Florida.

Jan. 26   ""   Arrived Panama City, for shakedown training.

Feb. 11   ""   Departed Panama City for New Orleans.

Feb. 12   ""   Arrive New Orleans.

Feb. 19   ""   Departed New Orleans for New York.

March 1   ""   Arrived at New York for loading.

March 5   ""   Departed New York for Boston.

~~March 6   ""   Arrive Boston.~~ *Did not stop at Boston*

March 10   ""   Departed Boston for Halifax, Nova Scotia.

~~March 12   ""   Arrived Halifax.~~

March 14   ""   Departed Halifax for Roseneath, Scotland.

March 31   ""   Arrive Roseneath.

April 2   ""   Departed Roseneath for Milford Haven, Wales.

April 3   ""   Arrived Milford Haven. Unloaded fuel oil.

April 5   ""   Departed Milford Haven, for Port Talbot.

April 6   ""   Arrive Port Talbot. Unloaded army equipment.

April 7   ""   Departed Port Talbot, for Falmouth, England.

April 9   ""   Arrive Falmouth.

Falmouth was assigned our home base. From there we made several trips to Brixham and back - took part in practice invasion.
This exercise gave us our first combat experience. During the nite of April 27, our convoy was attacked by German E boats. They sank two of our L.S.T.s and damaged the third. We landed on Slapton Sands, which is near Salcombe, England.
On June 5th, we left Brixham loaded with the army and equipment. This was the real invasion. On June 6th we arrived off Normandy about noon. Due to heavy fighting and rough seas we were unable to be unloaded until about 2:30 the 8th. At 8o'clock on the 8th, we started our return to England and at 9:05 we struck the mine that was the end of our L.S.T. and many fine friendships.

Mrs Richardson of the LST *499* (or M)

Copy of the schedule of LST-499, sent by Mrs Richardson, whose son served on that vessel, to Mrs Cantrell, mother of Ensign William Howard Cantrell, who perished on LST-531. *Copy courtesy of Beverly Hughes* away into the darkness. Within half an hour, however, the first torpedoes were fired on convoy T-4, narrowly missing LST-499, although at least one scraped along the shallow hull of LST-289.

For a while after this, nothing happened, but just before 01.30, LSTs 531 and 507 came under gunfire, tracers were spotted and General Quarters was sounded on most of the vessels. At this stage, the convoy was stretched out over three miles, with HMS Azalea just over a mile ahead. Meanwhile, back in Plymouth at almost exactly the same time, orders were issued to HMS *Saladin*—the nearest ship to the convoy at the time—to alter course and join up with T-4. However, she was thirty miles away from the convoy, which, unbeknown to anyone at Plymouth, was already under attack.

The gunfire attack seemed to be short-lived, as by 01.50 the firing had died down and some of the LSTs stood down from General Quarters, many believing this episode had all been a part of the exercise. Then, at 02.04, LST-507 was hit by a single torpedo, seemingly coming out of nowhere and she immediately caught fire, causing the other LSTs to take evasive action and alter course. Other vessels then returned to General Quarters, now beginning to understand that this was no drill. Meanwhile, Rescue Motor Launches were sent out from Portland. As they approached the convoy, the attack began in earnest and when the US sailors started firing at the E-boats, the RMLs were ordered back to port, for fear they would be mistaken for E-boats and fired upon.

Within fifteen minutes, LST-531 was also struck by two torpedoes in quick succession and began to lilt towards her starboard, losing all power and means of communication. The order was given to abandon ship and, as by now Commander Skahill on LST-515 had been made aware of the reality of the attack, he issued an order for the convoy to scatter. Just a few minutes after LST-531 was hit, LST-289 came under attack, but no immediate damage was done.

LST-531 started to sink only six minutes after the first torpedo strike, leaving the men on board with little chance of escape. Meanwhile, out in front of the convoy, Lieutenant Commander George Geddes of HMS *Azalea* sent a radio message to Portsmouth informing them that the convoy was under attack. Geddes was not really sure what was happening at this stage, but could clearly see burning ships in the water. At the same time, Skahill on LST-515 and the commanding officer of LST-499 also sent radio messages to Portland, saying that they were being attacked. There was some confusion here, as Skahill described the attackers (correctly) as E-boats, while the C.O. of LST-499 referred to them as U-boats. However, much more importantly, the Royal Navy and US Navy ships could not communicate with each other, and each was communicating with a different shore base in England, so no-one really had a clue what was going on, or who was responsible for what. At 02.30, Lieutenant James Swarts, captain of LST-507, gave the order to abandon ship, at almost exactly the same time as LST-289 came under renewed attack. She was hit in the stern, jamming the steering and causing considerable damage to her hull.

Just a few minutes later, the captain of LST-58, Lieutenant John Wachter decided to cast adrift the pontoon which he was towing to aid his vessel's escape from the area. The undamaged ships were scattering, as ordered, and heading for the coast.

By 02.45, LST-507 had been abandoned, with her executive officer, Lieutenant James Murdock and her captain, Lieutenant Swarts, being the last to leave. By this time, LST-507 was well alight and many of the men below decks burned to death. It took until 03.15 for the vessel to sink, but even then her bows remained above the water, until sunk later in the morning by HMS *Saladin*.

By now, the E-boats had withdrawn, but throughout the attack, men aboard the undamaged LSTs had fired their guns indiscriminately, sometimes hitting and injuring either their comrades on board other ships, or those in the water.

At approximately 05.00, LST-515 returned to the scene of the attack and began to pick up survivors. She was joined by HMS *Saladin* and HMS *Onslow*, which had initially gone after the E-boats, but had broken off the chase. HMS *Obedient* and HMS *Brissenden* also arrived on the scene to help search for the survivors, while the remaining LSTs anchored in West Bay to offload their own wounded before continuing on to Slapton Sands later that evening. HMS *Azalea* escorted LST-289 back to Dartmouth, where she arrived at 14.30. The Rescue Motor Launches were sent out from Portland again at first light, but there were no survivors left in the water by this time.

· · · · ·

The men on each side of the fighting forces gained a different perspective of events. Those on each LST sometimes saw the attack in a contrasting light to their comrades on another ship or to other witnesses of different nationalities. This is partly because the vessels on which they were travelling were spread out as a convoy, but is also because their experiences differed greatly as individuals, depending on which arm of the services they served with, and how they saw the E-boat attack. In addition, although a few of these personnel and detailed accounts were given at the time, or in the few weeks just after the exercise, most of them have been recounted in the last thirty years, which is to say, more than forty years after the events which are being described actually took place. In some cases, this has led to an element of confusion over timings, the sequence of events and, in certain instances, the personnel involved.

Lieutenant James Frederick Murdock served as the executive officer on board LST-*507*. In his account of the exercise, given on 16 August 1944, he recalls leaving Brixham on the afternoon of 27 April, with the ship carrying a full crew and 282 army personnel together with their equipment. Accompanying LST-*507* were LSTs *289* and *499*. He describes the conditions as 'being probably fairly good. The wind was from gentle to zero. A quarter moon was low and setting. The sea was calm, the visibility was fair to good.' These three vessels manoeuvred in the English Channel until joined by five other LSTs that had come up from Plymouth. Having fallen in astern of these five ships (with LST-*507* bringing up the rear), the convoy began their journey to Slapton Sands.

Murdock goes on to say that at approximately 01.35, gunfire was heard and General Quarters was sounded and, about ten minutes later he saw 'two apparently very fast ships to starboard'. No action was taken against these ships, because it was assumed that they were part of the convoy's escort. According to Lieutenant Murdock, the next thing that happened was that a torpedo struck the ship on the starboard, which 'tore through the sides and exploded in the near vicinity of the auxiliary engine room'. The explosion cut the power to the entire ship and caused fires on the 'tank deck, in the engine rooms and topside'. Gasoline caught fire, spreading across the decks and this 'poured into the fuel oil which was seeping out of the side of the ship'. This, in turn, caused fire on the water surrounding the vessel. With the bow of the ship 'entirely separated from the bridge and the stern-most part of the vessel', communications with anyone in the bow became impossible.

Lieutenant Murdock recalls that having tried to get the fires under control and, realising the gravity of the situation, the captain, Lieutenant James Swarts gave orders to throw all ammunition overboard to prevent any further explosions on board ship. Then, with the ship sinking by the stern as well as listing to starboard, the captain gave the order to abandon ship. According to Lieutenant Murdock, only two life rafts were useable and deployed—the remainder were either damaged by the fires or explosions, or they could not be reached because of the flames. The army personnel left by the stern, wearing life belts; navy personnel followed their drill and left from wherever on the ship they safely could, most of them wearing kapok life jackets, giving them a better chance of survival.

Another Naval man, Angelo Crapanzano, a Motor Machinist's Mate, First Class, on board LST-*507*, gave a rather more confused tale of the events of 27 and 28 April 1944. In his account, given in 1994, fifty years after the event, he recalls his vessel leaving port in the company of LST-*531* and another ship (which he does not identify), with an escort of 'two British Corvettes', which promptly both 'turned around and went back to England', leaving the convoy with no escort at all. Crapanzano had been given a tetanus booster shot the day before sailing and, just before going on duty in the engine room at midnight, he reported to the engineering officer that he felt unwell. He was sent to the Pharmacist's Mate, who found that Crapanazano had a temperature of 104 degrees, at which point he was ordered back to the crew's quarters to rest. Feeling quite unwell by this time, Crapanzano went to sleep on his bunk, but was woken again by the sound of the General Quarters alarm. Grabbing his life jacket, Crapanzano headed straight for the engine room, where his job was to log the changes in speed that were being ordered by the bridge. The last time that he remembers writing in the log was 02.03, when there was a 'terrific roar' and then 'everything went black'.

Although it was impossible to see anything, Crapanzano knew that a torpedo had struck the ship in the auxiliary engine room, just forward of where he was. Luckily for him, he also knew his way around the engine room, even in the pitch black and made for the escape ladder which was situated in one corner. In his account, Crapanzano recalls that, once on deck, he could see that the ship was on fire and 'split in half', burning 'from the bow to the wheelhouse'. He describes the soldiers on board as 'panicking' and jumping overboard without waiting for orders. Having been on deck for a short while, Crapanzano then saw LST-531 being struck by two torpedoes and sinking within 'about ten minutes'. After this, according to Crapanzano, another torpedo was fired at LST-507, missing by only 'ten or twelve feet'. Eventually the captain gave the order to abandon ship and Crapanzano knew that he had to jump quickly. The deck was getting hot, because the tank deck below was burning fiercely but, when he looked over the side, he saw that the sea was also on fire and there were lots of other men already in the water. He worried that he might jump into the flames and land on top of one of his comrades and then, possibly, have someone else jump in on top of him. Despite his fears, Crapanzano made up his mind to jump.

Having completed his intensive training, Patsy Giacchi found himself on board LST-507, along with his comrades from the 557th Quartermaster Railhead Company, whose job it was to keep the front-line troops supplied. Giacchi and his fellow soldiers were told to make themselves as comfortable as possible on board the ship, so he and his friend Patty Moreno found two stretchers in the corner of the well-lit tank deck and began to settle down.

The first thing that Giacchi recalls in his account of the attack, given in 1998, was the sound of scraping, which was followed by the sight of 'little puddles of water where the big doors are'. Giacchi, sensing that something was wrong, started to panic and yelled to Moreno that they should go up on deck. Moreno, however, decided to stay where he was, commenting that they were only on a 'dry run', so nothing could really be wrong. Giacchi was not so certain and, grabbing his helmet and life belt, he climbed up the steps to the deck.

Just before going, Giacchi remembers glancing around him and seeing 'guys shooting dice, playing cards … a thousand soldiers'. When he got up on deck, Giacchi recalls seeing that the 'ocean was on fire'. He had been followed up the steps by another soldier, named Bradshaw, but according to Giacchi, they had barely had time to take in the sight before them, when the ship was hit. Both men were thrown into the air and, when Giacchi fell, he landed on a 'piece of sharp, square metal'. He then 'started to bleed' from his head. Despite this injury, he was alive, as was Bradshaw and they both knew they must get off the ship, sooner rather than later.

Like Patsy Giacchi, Lieutenant Eugene Eckstam had completed his training, but he was still feeling ill-prepared for what lay ahead, when he boarded LST-507 as part of her medical unit, codenamed Foxy 29. Years later, he would recall the loading of 'some 290 army personnel', together with their vehicles, which took place at Brixham, commencing on 24 April. Once the ship had departed the dock, Eckstam recalls the army men 'sitting around on the decks eating their rations out of tins'. He describes them all as sailing along in 'fatal ignorance' in the Channel, when everyone was roused at 01.30 by the sounding of General Quarters, followed by the noise of gunfire.

Eckstam remembers that he was attempting to go 'topside' at 02.03, when the ship was hit, causing all the lights to go out. In his role as physician, Eckstam went to the ward room, where several wounded men had been taken, but seeing that there were enough medics there to take care of these men, Eckstam went below to see if he could be of any help. When he reached the tank deck, he opened the hatch and found himself 'looking into a raging inferno', into which he could not possibly enter. He also knew that, under Navy regulations, the hatch must be closed again so, despite the screams of the men inside, that is exactly what he did. The order to abandon ship was given at 02.30 and, rather than jumping over the side of the ship, Eckstam recalls 'climbing down a cargo net' and lowering himself into the numbingly cold water.

Ed Panter served with Eugene Eckstam in Foxy 29 but, interestingly, he has a rather different recollection of abandoning LST-507 in that he describes himself and Eckstam as jumping 'off the stern' and 'swimming away from the ship'.

Petty Officer Steve Sadlon was asleep when he heard a scraping sound along the 'side' of LST-507 and then General Quarters was sounded 'a moment later', whereupon he 'ran for the radio shack'. He had barely had time to sit down in his chair, when the torpedo struck the auxiliary engine room, immediately below where Sadlon was sitting. The force of the explosion threw him out of his seat and he was knocked unconscious. When he came to, 'all hell was breaking loose aboard ship'. The fires were out of control, ammunition and gas canisters were exploding and 'sailors were running all over the place'. Once the order was given to abandon ship, Sadlon made his way to the stern, where he found other soldiers and sailors. Among them was a signalman who looked down into the burning water below and declared to Sadlon that he had no intention of jumping in. Sadlon recalls looking around and says that he pointed out to the signalman that the alternative was stay where they were and burn to death. Sadlon jumped in, but as far as he could recall, the signalman remained on board LST-507 and died

Ensign Douglas Harlander was on duty in the chart house of LST-531 when LST-507 was struck. He watched 'fearfully' as the flames engulfed her and the surrounding waters. Upon leaving Plymouth several hours earlier, Harlander had wondered, in common with many others on board, whether this time, they were embarking for the 'real thing'—the actual invasion into France—rather than just another practice. However, when the orders had been opened by Lieutenant John Behrens, Commanding Officer of LST-531, Harlander and everyone else on board had quickly realised that this was, indeed, a 'dry run'. The sight of one of the other LSTs on fire, during what was only supposed to be an exercise, filled him with horror. He had barely had time to take on board what was happening, when his own ship was struck by the first torpedo. He was thrown into the air, but was not hurt and went below to alert the troops. Upon finding an army captain asleep in his bunk, Harlander woke him and told him to get his men and go up on deck, before making his way topside himself. Just as Harlander reached the deck, the second torpedo struck the ship, ripping a hole in the side of her hull. Going to the port side main deck, he discovered that the ship was 'completely engulfed in flames', with the exception of the port side aft section. LST-531 immediately began to list to starboard and, as the most senior man around, he gave the order to abandon ship, although there were few to hear him.

One of the naval ratings on board LST-531, was John A. Brown, who served with Lieutenant John Hill and, a while after the attack, in 1945, he began writing to Hill's sister, Marion Irving. In his letters, Brown briefly describes the events of the early hours of 28 April. He recalls that the ship was fully loaded with army personnel and their material and that they sailed without 'alarm of any kind' until around 01.15, when General Quarters was sounded. At this point, Brown went to the engine room, where he was on duty with 'two more and Mr Hill'. This seemed to be a false alarm and they were stood down again at 01.45, whereupon Brown returned to bed and Hill went back to his own quarters. Then, between 02.05 and 02.10, Brown recalls that the first torpedo struck the ship, quickly followed by a second. He got up on deck as quickly as he could, where he got into a life raft. He did not see Lieutenant Hill again.

Letter from John A. Brown, who served on LST-*531*, to Marion Irving, aunt of Lieutenant John H. Hill Jr. *Letter courtesy of Beverly Hughes*

Another naval man who wrote to Lieutenant Hill's family, was Ensign Raymond Gosselin. He sent his correspondence to John Hill's wife, Florence, who lived in Boston, with their twelve year old son, Robert. Gosselin only vaguely describes 'contact with the enemy', saying that 'after some action, we were torpedoed and sank rapidly'. Gosselin explains that his leg was broken and that he had sustained other injuries as well as a result of the explosions, which made his own escape difficult. He describes only seeing Lieutenant Hill prior to the ship being struck by the first torpedo, but not afterwards.

One of the soldiers on board LST-531, John A. Perry was serving with the 462nd Amphibious Truck Company and was asleep in one of the DUKWs (an amphibious truck), when the ship was hit by the first torpedo. Grabbing his gas mask, he managed to make it onto the deck, but was struck in the legs and fell overboard, seemingly unaware of what was happening around him.

From on board LST-289, the attack looked rather different. At 01.30, her commanding officer, Lieutenant Harry Mettler noticed gunfire, which seemed to be directed at LST-507, the ship immediately behind his own. No enemy vessels had been sighted and, uncertain whether this was a real attack, or part of the exercise, Mettler continued as he would have done under attack circumstances and sounded General Quarters. At that stage, no gunners on LST-289 opened fire, because they had not sighted the enemy. Then, at 02.30, Mettler heard the explosion that signalled the first torpedo strike, against LST-507 and, realising that this was definitely no exercise, he contemplated stopping to pick up survivors. However, he quickly changed his mind, as the exact source of the enemy fire was still unknown, so to stop his own vessel would endanger his crew and the lives of the 395 soldiers on board.

Further torpedo wakes were spotted in the water and, as one approached LST-289, Mettler gave the order to take evasive action. Gunners began firing at the torpedo and it seemed as though it might pass just behind the ship, but it did not and struck her, above the water line, just forward of her stern. The noise was considerable, given that it was not muffled by the water and the damage was significant, but not as severe as on LSTs 507 and 531. The engines stopped and the steering was impaired, but Mettler's immediate priorities were to control the fires and flooding. Consideration was given as to whether to try to get the army personnel off the ship, being as the 478th Amphibious Truck Company had the means to do this. Their Commanding Officer approached Mettler and suggested that they could lower the LST ramps and drive off the DUKWs, loaded with men, then head for the shore. This was a dangerous proposition, given that there were still unidentified enemy vessels in the vicinity, but Mettler was also faced with the very real prospect, at that stage, that his ship might sink. However, the fires and floods were brought under control before a final decision had to be taken, so the soldiers remained on board. Power was regained, but LST-289 could not be steered properly, so Mettler decided to lower five LCVPs (Landing Craft Vehicle/Personnel) into the water, which ran alongside and steered the ship back to port. Mettler was ordered to return to Brixham, but he refused, knowing that there were no medical facilities there. He insisted instead, on sailing to Dartmouth, arriving there on the afternoon of 28 April, where the dead and wounded were disembarked,

Pl S. My mother is ~~NXXXX~~ Mrs. I. M. Gosselin
346 Coolidge Ave., Manchester, N.H.
Copy of letter received from
Ensign R. A. Gosselin   July 6th

Dear Mrs. Hill:

I was very pleased to hear from you
as I have been wanting to drop you a line
ever since that fateful day of April 28th.
I knew your husband very well as we
are both from N. E. My home is in Manchester, N.H. and have spent a good deal of
time in and around Boston. He was a fine
man and was very well liked by everyone aboard
the ship.
He did all his own work and then helped
the others out on their work too.
Soon after we arrived in England, we
went on exercises and on one such exercise
we made contact with the enemy and after
some action, we were torpedoed twice and
sank rapidly. The last time I saw John was
earlier that evening before the action began.
One of the handful of survivors said he saw
him after we were hit, and he seemed alright,
but no one has since seen him.
I broke my leg and got a few minor
wounds and managed as best I could to swim to
a raft after the ship had gone down. There
were several men there already, and I picked
up several others afterwards, those were the
only ones I found. Mr. Hock did about the
same on another raft.
Mr. Hock expects to be back in the
States soon and said he would try and see
you if at all possible. I am going back to
duty over here soon. But if and when I get
home, I 'll certainly call on you and talk
it all over with you.
I'm very sorry about John, Mrs. Hill
and know how badly you, his mother and sisters
must feel.
Sincerely
Ensign R. A. Gosselin

Letter from Ensign Raymond A. Gosselin, who served on LST-*531*, to Mrs Florence
Hill, widow of Lieutenant John H. Hill Jr. Letter courtesy of Beverly Hughes.

the latter being taken to 228th Station Hospital at Sherborne. In his report, Mettler was full of praise for the conduct of his own crew and also the army personnel on board LST-289, who took over some of the naval duties when the crewmen manned the LCVPs to steer the ship back to Dartmouth.

LST-515 was the command vessel for convoy T-4. Her commanding officer was Lieutenant John Doyle, but also on board was Commander Bernard Skahill, who was the Commodore of T-4 and outranked Doyle. The two men had slightly different agendas and purposes. For Doyle, his primary concerns were the well-being of his ship, her crew and their 'passengers' of army personnel. Skahill, on the other hand, was more interested in the convoy and the exercise as a whole. This conflict of interests led to some clashes between the two men that would become much more significant in the early hours of 28 April. In recent years, some of the men who served on board the ship have come forward to say that they had always felt that Skahill lacked the qualities required to command the convoy, but this is something which is easier to say in hindsight, with the knowledge of what subsequently happened to T-4. There are others who maintain that he was a 'kind and gentle man', who expected bravery and commitment from his men. One seventeen-year-old quartermaster who served on LST-515 recalled in 1985, how Skahill 'reprimanded an LST captain for inching his ship out of place in a convoy into a less exposed position ... The message was hotly worded. I know, I was the one who sent it on the blinker'.

Unlike some of the other LST commanders, Lieutenant Doyle had ensured that his crew was properly trained and they spent much of their Atlantic crossing performing drills for various scenarios, such as collisions and abandoning the ship, so that they were well prepared for what was to come.

At 01.30, when the first gunfire was noticed, Commander Skahill was in bed. Lieutenant Moses Hallett, the ship's executive and communications officer decided that the situation was not serious enough to wake Skahill, as no enemy vessels had been sighted on the radar. Nonetheless, Doyle ordered the sounding of General Quarters as a precaution, only to have the men stood down again, roughly twenty minutes later at 01.55.

Within ten minutes, the first torpedo had struck, hitting LST-507 and Hallett now decided to wake Commander Skahill, who surveyed the scene that met him upon his arrival on the bridge. He could see a burning ship, some three miles astern of his own vessel; HMS *Azalea*, the convoy's escort, was still moving forward in front of the convoy and had not changed her course and there were no radio messages regarding an attack or any enemy vessels in the vicinity. Skahill decided, therefore, that the burning ship was unconnected with him and had nothing to do with his convoy. Although radar contacts were being made, these were written off as friendly vessels, so no action was taken at all. A few minutes later, however, a torpedo was sighted in the water and Doyle gave the order for the ship to make a sharp turn so that the torpedo narrowly missed their vessel. Just as Doyle was becoming convinced that the convoy was under genuine attack, everyone on board LST-515 not only heard, but also felt the explosion that shook LST-531. The radar contacts were now realised to be enemy E-boats and LST-515 opened fire, although her gunners could not aim with any degree of accuracy, because they could not see their targets.

By 02.24, Skahill was suitably convinced that the whole convoy was under threat and he ordered Hallett to contact Portland, notifying them of the assault. In accordance with the orders he had been given (which were standard convoy instructions), Skahill instructed the undamaged LSTs to scatter and head for the shore.

Although Lieutenant Doyle knew that Skahill was only following orders, he also knew that there would very probably be men still alive in the burning, yet freezing Channel waters. While heading for the shore, he and Skahill proceeded to argue for some time about whether to continue on their course as ordered, or turn around and go back for any survivors that might be left behind. According to one account, Doyle asked the crew of the LST, over the loudspeaker system, whether they wanted to save the ship (and themselves) by going to the shore, or whether they would prefer to stay behind and look for survivors, even though this might mean engaging the enemy in a dangerous battle, for which they were ill-equipped. He evidently received a resounding cheer of, 'Let's stay and fight'. Whether a seasoned and sensible naval officer like Doyle would have permitted the crew to make such a decision is dubious to put it mildly, and whether Skahill would have gone along with Doyle's course of action and paid any attention to its outcome is even more doubtful. What is certain, is that at 03.58, Doyle won the day and LST-515 turned back towards the scene of the attack, where she joined HMS *Saladin* in the search for survivors.

LST-511 was the third ship in the convoy and the first thing her crew knew of the attack was the sighting of gunfire to their stern, which they believed to be part of the exercise. Then, at just after 02.00, the men heard the explosion caused by the torpedo striking LST-507, but this was nothing compared to what happened next. The ship immediately behind LST-511 was LST-531 and when she was struck, the whole of LST-511 shook with the force of the explosion. Within minutes, while the men were still recovering from the shock of the scene unfolding before them, LST-289, four ships behind them, was hit and simultaneously, some men felt and heard a scraping of metal against their own ship's bow, which they believed to be an unexploded torpedo. An E-boat approached, passing between LST-511 and the ship immediately in front, which was LST-496 and the gunners on board this latter vessel, opened fire, raking the deck of LST-511 with a hail of bullets.

Clifford Graves was the medical officer on board LST-511, serving with Company D of 261st Medical Battalion. Having been on duty all day, he retired at midnight, only to be awoken at 02.00 when General Quarters was sounded. Thinking that this was part of the exercise, Graves was initially reluctant to get out of bed and get dressed, until one of the crew ran in and told him that this was not a practice, but the 'real thing'. Graves quickly got himself up on the deck, where he saw a 'large fire burning out in the Channel about a mile behind us'. Graves realised straight away that the burning ship was part of the convoy. Then the LST directly behind [LST-531] suddenly exploded and 'burst into a great mass of flame all at once'. At that point, LST-511 really came to life, as 'all hell started to break loose'. There was a great deal of confusion on board as the LST came under fire. Graves took shelter to start with and then made his way to the ward room. As he went down one of the ship's narrow corridors, he was accosted by a soldier who was clutching his stomach and crying out, 'I've been hit'. Upon first examining the man, Graves could find nothing wrong with him, until he undid his shirt and discovered that a fragment of shrapnel had sheared into the soldier's belly. Graves had the man taken to the ward room, in the middle portion of the ship, on the upper deck level and, once there, he set to work. Casualties came in thick and fast to begin with, until the gunners on board LST-496, who were firing indiscriminately at LST-511, realised their mistake and ceased firing. All in all, there were nineteen casualties for Graves and his team to deal with. However, even once the gunfire had stopped, the ship remained in imminent danger, initially from the E-boats and then, once they had departed, she had to negotiate her way past the mines, laid in the Channel, for which they had no charts.

Lieutenant Stanley Koch, the Commanding Officer of LST-496 was asleep at 01.30 when General Quarters was sounded. He was astounded at this intrusion: knowing that the crew would have to be up soon anyway, he could not believe that someone had decided that this was a good time for a drill. Upon reaching the bridge, he was told that gunfire tracers had been sighted to the stern of the ship. Koch ascertained that there were no radar contacts and at 01.53, the crew was stood down from General Quarters.

Just after 02.00, when LST-507 was struck, signalman Manny Rubin sighted burning oil on the water, as well as the ship aflame and men struggling in the sea, trying to escape. By now, the radar on board LST-496, the second ship in the convoy, was picking up various unidentified vessels.

When LST-531, which was two ships behind, was struck a few minutes later, Rubin saw an explosion, followed by intense flames and 'black specks' all around the edges of the fires, which he assumed to be parts of the ship, or vehicles, or even men, blown up into the air by the sheer force of the explosion. He would later describe the atmosphere on board LST-496 at this point as being one of fear and hysteria, noting that the army men were terrified that their ship might be the next one to be hit.

At 02.30, just after LST-289 was struck, an E-boat passed close by LST-496 and she came under fire, which strafed the bridge. Shrapnel pierced through Rubin's helmet, cutting his head. Having applied a dressing, he called down to Lieutenant Koch that he could see a bow-wave—presumably from an E-boat—approaching from the port side. One of the army men, on hearing this, opened fire with his machine gun and the gunners on LST-496 followed suit, believing they were under attack, but none of them realised that they were actually firing on LST-511 and wounding their comrades. It was only when they became aware of the fact that they were having to aim too high to be firing at an E-boat, that they understood their mistake and ceased firing. Lieutenant Koch received orders to head for the shore, which he did.

LSTs 499 and 58 were next to each other—fifth and sixth in the convoy. LST-58 was immediately behind LST-531 and was towing two pontoon causeways. In common with the other LSTs, both ships went to General Quarters at about 01.30, after tracer fire was spotted, but they stood down approximately twenty minutes later. At this stage, as far as these two ships were concerned, there was a lull in the action: nothing was sighted or heard until suddenly, the men on board LST-58 were surprised to see LST-499 change course, pulling out of position in the convoy, seemingly taking evasive action from a torpedo. Just after 02.00, when LST-507 was struck, General Quarters was sounded again aboard LST-58 and the army personnel aboard were ordered to the starboard messing compartments.

At 02.17 the men aboard LST-58 heard the engines of an E-boat, although at that time no vessel was sighted. Within minutes LST-531 exploded and began to sink right in front of LST-58, which was forced to pull to port to avoid the burning ship. However, this manoeuvre was hampered and made more difficult by the fact that LST-58 was still towing her two pontoons, making steering cumbersome and also, LST-499, having moved out of position, was now blocking her passage and had to move herself. At the time of the explosion on LST-531, the force was so great that many on board LST-58 believed that she too had been hit.

Then, at 02.25, LST-499 broke radio silence and sent a message to Portland explaining that the convoy was under attack by 'submarines'. Just after this, following orders received from Commander Skahill on LST-515, both LSTs scattered and headed towards the shore and at 03.00, LST-58 discarded both of the pontoons she was towing to ease her getaway.

John Maltese remembers various aspects of the night of the E-boat attack, with a degree of accuracy. In his account, given in September 2008, he does not say on which LST he served, but he also does not mention abandoning his ship, so we may assume that it was not LST-507 or 531. He served with the 462nd Amphibious Truck Company, the members of which were loaded onto various LSTs. His memory of Exercise Tiger is that the convoy left 'Dover' to travel to Slapton Sands, where the equipment would be offloaded onto the beach. He recalls that at 02.30, general quarters was sounded, but states that everyone thought this was part of the exercise and that the men were told to remain below deck.

. . . . .

Looking at the attack from a German perspective only really aids to confuse. There are at least four separate logs of events during the night of 27–28 April and these give details, which not only conflict with each other, but also with most of the American accounts.

Known to the Germans not as an E-boat, but as an S-boot (Schnellboot), the vessels that participated in the attack on the Exercise Tiger convoy T-4 came from the 5th S-Flottille and the 9th S-Flottille, based at Cherbourg. The boats were numbered as follows: S-*136, 138, 140, 142, 143* and *100* (from the 5th S-Flottille) and S-*130, 145* and *150* (from the 9th S-Flottille).

The officer commanding the 5th S-Flottille was Korvettenkapitän Bernd Klug. In his official log, he cited that his flotilla of six boats left Cherbourg at 22.00 on the night of 27 April. They had been ordered to intercept and take action against 'detected enemy targets' to the west of Portland Bill. At 00.05, their target was detected and the S-boote divided into pairs to make their attack. S-*138* and S-*136* reported a 'shadow' off their port bow and then, after a few minutes, Klug observed a 'very large detonation', followed by two flares 'very high in the sky', at which point he made the assumption that there were aircraft in the vicinity. He communicated with S-*136* by underwater telephone and asked what had caused the explosion, but received no response. At this stage, the S-boot commanders were convinced that they were attacking destroyers, so when they struck the LSTs and began to report them as sinking, the messages sent out at that stage related to 'destroyers', although they were also variously termed 'steamers' and 'tankers', as the attack progressed. Klug wanted to engage the other 'destroyers' in the area, so he ordered a change of direction and increased speed, proceeding north.

At 02.05, Klug's S-boot fired on a 'steamer', but this torpedo missed 'due to under-estimation of speed' of the 'steamer', which Klug estimated—quite accurately—to be around five knots. Another 'tanker' was observed at 02.03, further north. This vessel was 'burning brightly' and giving off a great deal of 'black smoke' which was covering the southern part of Lyme Bay. S-143 fired two torpedoes at 02.16, which struck another 'steamer'. Klug described the ship as sinking 'in flames'. The S-boote were now darting in and out of the 'destroyers', firing torpedoes at various times. Klug called off the attack at 03.17 due to increased traffic in the area, as well as the fact that S-143 had been 'struck in the stern', causing damage to her torpedo tubes. Klug stated that he was returning to port because he had no wish to subject his flotilla to additional danger.

The Commander of S-140 (part of the 5th S-Flottille) was Oberleutnant zur See Götschke, wrote in his official log, that between midnight and 01.13, several torpedoes were fired in the direction of the 'steamers', but that these all missed, probably due to the 'varying slow speed of the vessels'. However, he did admit that if the 'steamers' were actually Landing Craft Tanks, it was possible that the torpedoes were passing under their shallow hulls.

At 01.26, Götschke observed two torpedoes striking 'on land', then four minutes later, moved his vessel into position to attack two of the 'steamers' with artillery fire. He sent a radio message at 02.00, stating that there were only three vessels in the convoy (although he subsequently changed this entry in his log to reflect the fact that the final three ships must have separated from the remainder of the convoy, which he would have realised with hindsight). At 02.40, S-140 withdrew from the area.

Kapitänleutnant Jürgenmeyer was the commanding officer of S-136 (part of the 5th S-Flottille) and in his official log, he reported that at 00.09, there was a 'severe detonation with outbreak of fire', which was 'strongly felt on our boat'. Then a few minutes later, he reported 'simultaneous detonation of both torpedoes' from S-146 into the second 'destroyer'. By 00.22, both of these 'destroyers' were slowed or stopped and Jürgenmeyer observed 'flares and surface fires'. At this stage, the S-136 moved south east to avoid the burning wreckage and scattering 'destroyers', returning to the area at 00.35 to ensure that the 'destroyers' had sunk, or if they had not sunk, to fire on them again and sink them. At 00.50, Jürgenmeyer sent out a message saying that the 'destroyer' was sinking and five minutes later, the S-136 passed directly over the site of the torpedoing, reporting 'nothing sighted'. Jürgenmeyer decided to call off the attack at 01.56 and returned to Cherbourg at 03.09.

The Commander of the 9th S-boot Flottille was Kapitänleutnant Freiherr von Mirbach. In his log, he noted that at 00.03, he saw a 'brief brilliant light at 70 degrees' and later concluded that this must have been from the torpedo that struck the 'English destroyer', fired by S-138. Von Mirbach made few notes then, other than course alterations, until 01.34, when he reported coming under machine gunfire which, although assumed to be enemy (because

The commissioning ceremony of LST-531. *Images courtesy of Beverly Hughes*

Activity in harbour during build-up to Exercise Tiger. *Source: unknown*

Fully loaded LSTs in harbour. *Source: unknown*

LSTs loading in build-up to Exercise Tiger, showing LST-496 in the background. *Source: unknown*

LST-289 at sea. *Source: unknown*

Some children sitting on a fence overlooking the exercises at Blackpool Sands, Devon.
Photograph courtesy of US National Archives

One of the exercises at Slapton Sands, showing the off-loading of soldiers and equipment.
Photograph courtesy of US National Archives

The interior of an LST, showing a group of men in front of the open doors. *Photograph courtesy of US National Archives*

Off-loading LCVPs at Slapton Sands during the exercises. *Photograph courtesy of US National Archives*

Left: Vehicles loaded onto the deck of an LST. *Photograph courtesy of US National Archives*

Below: Off-loading troops at Slapton Sands. *Photograph courtesy of US National Archives*

LSTs unloading at Slapton Sands during exercises, 1944. *Source: unknown*

Artistic interpretation of the Exercise Tiger E-boat attack by Ted Archer, 1995.

Damage to stern of LST-289 following E-boat attack. *Source: unknown*

Damage to stern of LST-289 following E-boat attack. *Source: unknown*

Crew of S-*130* during boat commissioning. *Image courtesy Archiv Peter Schlichting*

Commissioning of S-*130*. *Image courtesy Archiv Peter Schlichting*

Oberleutnant zur See Gunter Rabe—Captain of S-*130*. *Image courtesy Archiv Peter Schlichting*

Brookwood Cemetery. *Image courtesy of Beverly Hughes*

*Below, left:*Lieutenant John H. Hill Jr., from Boston, Massachusetts, who perished on LST-*531*. *Image courtesy of Beverly Hughes*

Below, right: Grave marker of Lieutenant John Hill Jr at Brookwood Cemetery. *Image courtesy of Beverly Hughes*

Left: Allen Obe Achey Jr. (Motor Machinist's Mate, Third Class), from Georgia, who perished on LST-*531*. *Image courtesy of Beverly Hughes*

Right: : Bernard Anthony Hauber (Electrician's Mate, Second Class), from Missouri, who perished on LST-*531*. *Image courtesy of Beverly Hughes*

Left: James J. Brown, who served in the US Navy on board LST-*531* and survived, although he was wounded. *Image courtesy of Beverly Hughes*

Right: Ensign William Howard Cantrell, from Kansas, who perished on LST-*531*. *Image courtesy of Beverly Hughes*

Left: William Wheeler Cobern (Motor Machinist's Mate, Third Class), from Alabama, who perished on LST-531. *Image courtesy of Beverly Hughes*

Right: Michael J, Coyle (Baker, Third Class), from Pennsylvania, who perished on LST-531. *Image courtesy of Beverly Hughes*

Left: Ensign Archer Frederick Cram, from Ohio, who perished on LST-531. *Image courtesy of Beverly Hughes*

Right: Ensign Archer F. Cram. *Image courtesy of Beverly Hughes*

Left: Robert Joseph Hartman (Radioman, Third Class), from Ohio, who perished on LST-*531*. *Image courtesy of Beverly Hughes*

Right: William Joseph Czerwinski (Fireman, First Class), from New York, who perished on LST-*531*. *Image courtesy of Beverly Hughes*

Left: Edwin James Dobson (Seaman, First Class), from Florida, who perished on LST-*531*. *Image courtesy of Beverly Hughes*

Right: Ensign Raymond A. Gosselin, who was wounded during the E-boat attack on LST-*531*, but survived. *Image courtesy of Beverly Hughes*

Left: Samuel D. Holmes (Motor Machinist's Mate, Second Class), from Florida, who perished on LST-*531*. *Image courtesy of Beverly Hughes*

Right: Brookwood grave markers of Samuel D. Holmes (left) and Cornelius Judson Parker, who both perished on LST-*531*. *Image courtesy of Beverly Hughes*

Left: Frederick J. Krause, who served on LST-*507* and survived the E-boat attack, although he was wounded. *Image courtesy of Beverly Hughes*

Right: Grave marker of Lester Harold Levy at Brookwood Cemetery (left). Levy, a Lieutenant from Pennsylvania perished on LST-*531*. *Image courtesy of Beverly Hughes*

Left: mery Eugene Marcus Jr., (Ship's Cook, Third Class), from Florida, who perished on LST-531. *Image courtesy of Beverly Hughes*

Right: Emery E. Marcus Jr. *Image courtesy of Beverly Hughes*

Left: Henry Victor Martin Jr., who served on LST-507 and was wounded in the E-boat attack. *Image courtesy of Suzan Martin Cunningham*

Right: Brookwood Cemetery grave marker of Doyle David Montgomery (Yeoman First Class), from North Carolina, who perished on LST-531. *Image courtesy of Beverly Hughes*

Left: Cornelius Judson Parker (Motor Machinist's Mate, Second Class), from Mississippi, who perished on LST-531. *Image courtesy of Beverly Hughes*

Right: Grave marker of William Pear (Electrician's Mate, Third Class), from New York, who perished on LST-531. *Image courtesy of Beverly Hughes*

Left: Albert Jerome Vendeland (Seaman, First Class), from Ohio, who perished on board LST-531. *Image courtesy of Beverly Hughes*

Right: Brookwood Cemetery grave markers of Albert Jerome Vendeland and Ensign John James Gallagher from Pennsylvania. Both men perished on LST-531. *Image courtesy of Beverly Hughes*

the tracer was red), turned out to be from S-*140* of the 5th S-boot Flottille, who were also using red tracer.

At 02.00, von Mirbach reported a torpedo strike, causing a 'steamer' to burst into 'bright flames'. He claimed that no defensive action was taken by the enemy vessels. Then at 02.17, a second steamer was struck by two torpedoes, which 'burst into flames immediately'. Von Mirbach referred to this as 'one of the most capable of all the attacks'. At 02.19, having observed the sinking of both ships, von Mirbach retreated from the scene, coming under heavy fire and returning to Cherbourg at 05.15. Later, he would attribute the sinking of the LSTs to S-*150* and S-*130* (LST-*531*), S-*150* (LST-*507*) and the torpedoing of LST-*289* was attributed by von Mirbach to S-*145*.

Oberleutnant zur See Gunter Rabe was the commanding officer of S-*130* and his recollections of the early hours of 28 April, rather than coming from an official log, recorded at the time, were recounted in 1985. He remembered that he, in company with the other boats in the 9th S-Flottille were headed towards Lyme Bay and had managed to approach the convoy without sighting any other ships or escort. A little before 02.00, they saw 'shadows of a long line of ships', which they could not identify, but which they presumed to be tankers or destroyers. According to Rabe, each vessel in the flotilla fired off two torpedoes, but none of them hit their targets, leading their commanders to believe that the targets must be shallow hulled ships, possibly LSTs. Rabe then fired off two further torpedoes aimed at the final ship in the convoy. Seconds later, there was a massive explosion, which Rabe attributed to his own torpedo strike, although he later learned that another S-boot had fired a torpedo at the same time as his own vessel.

A transcription of a German summary document of the attack, provides an overview of the event, written shortly afterwards. In this account, it is noted that the convoy had 'passed the Bill of Portland' at 21.00 (on 27 April) and that the S-boot Flottille came upon a 'landing training group which was only covered by destroyers at a distance'. The S-boote were able to pass by the escort 'almost without resistance'. In this German account, it is noted with some surprise that the escort was aware of the presence of the S-boote, but did nothing to protect or defend the convoy, or 'withdraw it from the attack area'. It is stated that the easternmost S-boot group 'attacked two presumed destroyers and torpedoed one of them', at which point the convoy broke up and 'sailed around relatively helplessly'. The convoy seemed to the Germans to be ponderous and 'poorly coordinated'.

The writer of this report states that the German boats 'suffered no losses' and that this may be 'attributed to the successful element of surprise'. At the time the Germans believed that they had sunk two American LSTs and torpedoed an LCT, which returned to Dartmouth. There is mention of a destroyer being sunk off 'the Bill of Portland', although the document states that this 'cannot be confirmed from the radio reports'. In this report, the sinking of LST-*531* is attributed to S-*136* and S-*138*.

Not only do these accounts disagree, to a certain extent, with the American versions of events, but there are also several anomalies between the different S-boot commanders' accounts of what happened. The first and most curious issue surrounds the explosion that is described as taking place just after midnight, described by possibly Jürgenmeyer, but definitely Klug and von Mirbach, which preceded the attacks on the LSTs *531*, *507* and *289*. There is no reference to this within the American accounts of the event, although it may be that this is the 'destroyer' mentioned in the German summary account, whose sinking could 'not be confirmed'. The fact that two high ranking and experienced officers described the same event, but that no-one else mentioned it, is very peculiar. Götschke—the commanding officer of S-*140*—mentions two torpedoes striking on land at 01.26, but again there is no American account of this and, indeed, no British version of events includes this account, which is also not detailed in the German summary.

Jürgenmeyer's timings for the torpedoing and sinking of the two LSTs are at variance with the other S-boot logs, in that he describes these as happening at just after midnight, rather than just after 02.00, which implies some confusion with the earlier detonation described by Klug and von Mirbach.

In addition, each S-boot commander attributes the torpedoing and sinking of the LSTs to different S-boote, none of which is really confirmed in the official summary.

None of these inconsistencies mean that any of the commanders was lying, or being wilfully obstructive; it simply suggests that in a situation of intense action such as this, everyone will have a different recollection of events.

· · · · ·

From a British perspective, there is significantly less to say, since the Royal Navy—although theoretically 'on hand'—were relative late-comers to the event.

The escort vessel, HMS *Azalea*, was commanded by Scotsman Lieutenant Commander George C. Geddes, who was familiar with escorting convoys and protecting them from the threat of submarine attacks, but had less experience with surface assaults by the enemy. HMS *Azalea* joined the convoy at 11.00 on 27 April, initially in company with HMS *Scimitar*. However, when *Scimitar* was ordered back to Plymouth due to damage to her hull, Geddes wrongly assumed that this action had been reported to Commander Skahill, the commodore of convoy T-4 aboard LST-515. This was especially the case when Geddes heard nothing to the contrary from Skahill himself, questioning the disappearance of HMS *Scimitar*, although that in itself is hardly surprising, as the two ships were using different radio frequencies. It appears that no-one, from the top down, had even thought that the two commanders might need to communicate with each other, so their frequencies were never co-ordinated by either them, or their superiors.

So, as the lone escort, HMS *Azalea* was steaming ahead of the convoy at a distance of just over one mile, when at 19.00, she received a message from Plymouth stating that there were E-boats in the area. This coded message took a while to decipher, by which time, the German vessels had already made their move. At 01.30 on 28 April, Lieutenant Commander Geddes sighted tracers, although this was at such a distances from HMS *Azalea* that Geddes was uncertain whether it was anything to do with the convoy at all.

By 02.25, everything had changed. Geddes had sighted two LSTs burning in the distance. He turned back and zigzagged along the starboard side of T-4. He was completely unaware from which side the E-boat attack had come and was, therefore, reluctant to send up flares to light the scene, for fear that this might silhouette the convoy and aid the attacking craft. As the *Azalea* drew nearer, one of the LSTs opened fire, believing her to be an E-boat and not long after this, the *Azalea* made radar contact with one enemy vessel, but she managed to escape. By the time HMS *Azalea* had reached the scene of the fires, other vessels were on hand to help survivors, so Geddes decided to accompany the remaining LSTs to the shore, as was his duty as the convoy's only escort vessel, before returning to oversee LST-289 on her journey back to Dartmouth.

Meanwhile, back in Plymouth, the belated order was issued at 01.37 to Lieutenant-Commander P. E. King, the commander of HMS *Saladin*, to pursue the convoy as a replacement escort for the damaged HMS *Scimitar*. By this time, however, convoy T-4 had already been sighted by the E-boats and was coming under gunfire. Not long after HMS *Saladin* received these orders, King saw tracer fire and then flames shooting high into the air. Realising that a ship had been hit, he altered course, heading in the direction of the flames and made haste. Unfortunately, the *Saladin*'s number one boiler was unreliable, so she was only capable of making twenty-three knots, but had nearly thirty miles to cover. At 02.25 King spotted further tracer fire and decided to pursue the enemy vessels that had started to appear on his radar. Almost immediately, however, he changed his mind, remembering that there were two vessels on fire and knowing that his first duty was to protect the convoy, he belayed his original order and headed back towards the fires, arriving at 03.15, where he found the half-submerged wreckage of LST-507.

The other burning vessel had disappeared.

The medical officer on board HMS *Saladin* was J. B. Wilson and he later recalled that there were 'hundreds' of bodies in the water, most of whom were still wearing their life jackets, but had their faces in the water. There were approximately fifty men clinging to the wreckage of LST-507 and these were picked up by HMS *Saladin*. Once these men were rescued, she fired her four-inch guns at the half-submerged wreck to sink her. Not long afterwards, LST-515 was reported arriving on the scene and she also began picking up survivors.

At 00.11, just before HMS *Saladin* was ordered to the scene, HMS *Onslow* was patrolling off of Portland Bill, when she sighted an E-boat heading in a northerly direction and, a little later, picked up three further groups of enemy vessels on her radar. These sightings were reported to Lieutenant Commander Geddes on HMS *Azalea*. HMS *Onslow* went in pursuit of these E-boats, but lost contact with them and eventually gave up the chase. She headed towards the scene of the attack and helped with picking up survivors and dead from the water.

Second Coxswain John Cullen was serving on board His Majesty's Rescue Motor Launch 532, based at Portland Dockyard. In May 2003 he would recall that his vessel was one of six boats ordered into Lyme Bay 'where an American convoy was in danger of attack by German E-boats'. The motor launches left their dock and headed out to sea. Throughout their journey, they were in constant contact with HMS *Attack*, which was a shore-based establishment set on top of Portland Bill, that had a panoramic view of the English Channel. With about fifteen miles left to cover, Cullen noticed 'gun flashes reflected by the low cloud, then some flares, followed later by some large explosions'. Being as the radio operator on board HMRML 532 could not contact the American ships, the vessel relied on HMS *Attack* for her information and was informed that the convoy had come under attack, being told that two ships had been sunk and one severely damaged. Now only five minutes from the convoy, the crew made ready to take on survivors, but then came under fire from the LSTs themselves. The captain of HMRML 532, Commander Scott, had to make a decision: should he stay and try to help the survivors, or leave the area and protect his own craft and crew? He reported the situation to HMS *Attack* and awaited their decision.

Elsewhere, Peter Nevill, a fighter-bomber pilot with the Royal Air Force Volunteer Reserve, was flying Beaufighters out of an airstrip in South Devon. On 27 April, he had celebrated his twentieth birthday and that night, went on patrol, flying in a loop as far east as the Isle of Wight, north to St David's and west to Land's End. While passing over Lyme Bay at 02.00, he saw a ship 'ablaze' and reported this to his controller, who told him to 'keep clear

… it's only an exercise'. Disobeying this order, Nevill circled the bay and his navigator then spotted fast moving vessels on his radar. Nevill dropped down for a look and quickly realised that he was 'being fired upon' by E-boats in the water below. Nevill fired two rockets, one of which hit an E-boat, 'setting it ablaze' and he recalls pursuing this vessel 'until it exploded'.

This report, like almost all of the others, is uncorroborated and stands contrary to the German summary document, which states that none of their vessels were damaged during the operation. However, Korvettenkapitän Klug had declared in his official log that S-*143* had been 'struck in the stern', citing this as one of the reasons for calling off the attack. This may account for some of Nevill's version of events, but nowhere does anyone else suggest that one of the E-boats 'exploded'. Equally, although Klug stated that he believed there were aircraft in the area, this report was entered into Klug's log at just after midnight, not at 02.00 when Nevill was in the vicinity and no E-boat commander claims to have shot at an aircraft.

These variations in the recollections of the event not only related to the attack itself, but also to the aftermath and what would happen to the men, both dead and alive, after the E-boats had done their worst.

CHAPTER SIX

'When Johnny Comes Marching Home'

The immediate aftermath of the attack and the stories of the survivors

There were several aspects that made a difference to each man's chances of survival in the immediate aftermath of the torpedo strikes on convoy T-4 in the early hours of 28 April 1944. One of the most important factors was which LST he had been on in the first place. Those on board LST-531 had approximately six minutes between the striking of the first torpedo and the sinking of the ship, giving them little chance of escape, especially if they were below deck at the time. Army losses were, therefore, especially high on that vessel, as most of the soldiers were on the tank deck trying to sleep. LST-507 stayed afloat for longer, but during that time, she burned fiercely and so did many of the men on board. Those who could get on deck, regardless of which ship they were on, faced the problems of jumping into freezing cold water, surrounded by burning oil and gasoline and seeing other men, some of whom had become their friends, dying in front of them, victims of the icy cold, oil-laden seas.

The survivors were picked up by several ships, including LST-515, which arrived back on the scene following the decision of her commanding officer, Lieutenant John Doyle, to defy the commodore of the convoy, Commander Bernard Skahill, and turn the ship around, rather than heading for port. Other ships participating in the rescue of survivors from the sea were HMS *Saladin* (the replacement for HMS *Scimitar*), HMS *Onslow*, HMS *Obedient* and HMS *Brissenden* although some of these vessels had also initially chased after the E-boats and then attempted to provide a screen against any further enemy attacks.

The commander of LST-507, Lieutenant James Swarts, having given the order to abandon ship at 02.30, was the last man to leave the ship, according to the account of his Executive Officer, Lieutenant James Murdock. In his report of the E-boat attack on convoy T-4, given in an interview on 16 August

1944, just over eleven weeks after the event had taken place, Murdock states that he and Swarts had left the ship at approximately 02.40, at which point the two men tried to 'get away from the fire spreading on the water'. Murdock also recalls that just over half an hour later, at 03.15, he noticed that most of the ship had disappeared beneath the water, leaving just her bow visible, which was later sunk, 'possibly by one of the destroyers which came up, by firing shells into her bow'.

Murdock and Swarts swam to a life raft, which already contained roughly ten men, including five naval officers, four naval crew and one army man. They paddled away from the ship and remained in the water until 06.00, when they saw LST-515 approaching and 'signalled to her with a flashlight', as well as shouting to attract the attention of her crew. Unfortunately, by this time, the soldier had already died from exposure and, just as they reached LST-515, one of the naval officers also blacked out and 'slipped off the raft'. The remaining men tried to rescue him, but he drowned before they could haul him back onto the raft. The rest of the survivors were taken on board LST-515, where they were given basic first aid and warm clothing. However, despite making it onto the LST, Lieutenant Swarts died shortly afterwards from the effects of shock and exposure.

For Petty Officer Angelo Crapanzano, also aboard LST-507, the decision to jump into the water was not really a difficult one. While he was worried about his landing and the flames licking on the surface of the water, the heat rising from the tank deck beneath him and the prospect of being on board a sinking ship were enough for him to make up his mind. He climbed up on top of the guard rail and jumped approximately forty feet into the water below, sinking 'a good six, eight feet' underneath the surface, before coming up for air. Going overboard with him was his friend, storekeeper, John T. McGarigal, who had a badly cut head, as a result of being blown 'from one side of the wheelhouse to the other' during the explosion when the torpedo struck the ship. Crapanzano's initial reaction, upon hitting the water, was confusion. Neither he nor McGarigal knew what they should do next, or what had happened to them and, still believing this to be a 'dry run', simply could not understand how their ship could have come under attack.

Once he had become more acclimatised to being in the water, Crapanzano then noticed a fire-damaged life raft floating towards him and McGarigal. Although there was not enough of the raft left to climb onto, the two men clung to its edges and were soon joined by 'nine soldiers', making eleven men in total. As the only fit naval man around the raft, Crapanzano took charge, telling the others that they must 'kick like hell' to 'get away from the ship', because he knew that remaining too close to the sinking vessel might cause them to be sucked down with it, when it sank. They also needed to escape as quickly as possible from the flames, which were continuing to spread across the water. As instructed, the men kicked away until they were outside the danger zone and then they clung onto the life raft and watched the sinking ship.

Having made it to relative safety, Crapanzano then became more aware of his immediate surroundings and was stunned by what he saw. In the water around him were 'hundreds' of bodies. Some were drowned, with their heads down in the water, because they were wearing their inflatable life belts incorrectly around their waists, rather than up under their arms. Some men had jumped overboard wearing their full packs and carrying rifles, so they could not stay afloat, even with their life belts on. More disturbing and shocking than these sights, however, were the men who had been burned. Crapanzano describes them as being 'stuck together and charred ... all black'. He believed that they had dived into the flaming water together and burned into a mass. Some may have been burned before jumping into the water, but in the darkness, it was impossible to tell. Most of the men either drowned, or succumbed to hypothermia, but others around the life raft were clearly victims of the actual torpedo explosion itself, with limbs missing and obvious evidence of physical trauma. The shock of witnessing these sights was as numbing as the freezing waters in which Crapanzano and his comrades now fought for their own survival.

After more than an hour in the water, Crapanzano could no longer feel his legs any more and, aware that the other men would probably be feeling the same, he urged them to keep kicking their legs and to stay awake, no matter how exhausted they got—even if they became desperate to sleep. Another hour passed and, not surprisingly, the men were becoming more and more tired and hopeless. Three of the soldiers discussed the situation and decided they were going to try to swim for the shore and, despite Crapanzano's protests that their idea was 'crazy', they ignored his pleas to remain with the life raft and went. They were followed by an army lieutenant who, in Crapanzano's words, 'went completely berserk' and pushed off from the raft, leaving only five soldiers, Crapanzano and McGarigal.

As the hours passed by, one by one, the soldiers just fell asleep, relinquishing their grip on the life raft and slipping below the surface of the water, until the only men left were Crapanzano and McGarigal. By now it was almost dawn and Crapanzano was having to hold onto McGarigal with one hand, while clinging to the life raft with the other, because McGarigal was now unconscious, due partly to the cold, but also to the wound on his head.

According to Crapanzano, after a total of about four-and-a-half hours in the water, just as he was beginning to give up hope of being rescued, he saw a light in the distance 'going up and down' and as he watched, the light became larger. He quickly realised that this meant an approaching ship and he knew that help was at hand. With an overwhelming sense of relief, Crapanzano finally succumbed to exhaustion and blacked out. He was quite literally too fatigued to stay awake any longer, having kept himself and McGarigal afloat for so long.

The next memory that Crapanzano recalls is of waking up in a bunk on board LST-515, headed for England and hospital. However, in later years, Crapanzano made contact with one of the men from LST-515, who had helped to rescue him. This man, Joe McCann, recalled Crapanzano easily because, despite his exhaustion, he had been 'mumbling' about his legs. During a conversation between the two men, McCann revealed that Crapanzano had nearly been left for dead. McCann had been on board a smaller vessel—one of two lowered by LST-515—and had passed by Crapanzano and McGarigal, believing them to be dead, when someone had noticed that Crapanzano appeared to move. They turned the boat around and went back, picking up both men and taking them back to LST-515.

Once Crapanzano arrived in England, he and his fellow survivors were treated in hospital and he was told that there would be no long-term effects from his ordeal. Then, the men were divided up into smaller sections and put into what Crapanzano refers to as 'isolation camps', although the authorities called them 'rest camps'. According to Crapanzano, the men were expecting to be given some leave and, possibly even some time back home in the US after what they had been through, but instead they were kept confined to the camp and were told to speak to absolutely no-one about what had happened.

Three weeks later, Crapanzano and the men he was with, were told that they would be taking part in the invasion into Northern France. The men were incredulous. They had a better understanding than most of what lay ahead for them; they had been through a terrible and terrifying experience and now they were being asked to do it all over again—only this time, everyone knew for certain that this was no practice—this time it was for real.

Meanwhile, Patsy Giacchi, still bleeding from the injury to his head, had taken no time at all to make the decision to jump off LST-507. Taking the hand of his comrade, Bradshaw, the two men jumped together, roughly forty feet into the icy seas beneath them. Both men had already inflated their life belts and pulled them up around their chests. According to Giacchi and contrary to the statements of many other participants in the exercise, he and his group did receive perfectly adequate training in the use of these life belts and it was explained to them how they should be inflated and worn. Although Giacchi obviously could not be expected to speak for anyone else involved in Exercise Tiger and he could not have any knowledge of the training given to other groups, his own view was that some of the men who did not use their belts properly, were panicking, rather than badly trained.

Having hit the water, the first thing that the two men became aware of was the cold, followed by an overwhelming smell of oil and gasoline. Giacchi then began to notice the men in the water around him. Most of them were already dead, some with missing limbs, others had clearly drowned. He heard the cries of wounded men, begging for help, even though there was none to be had. Giacchi and Bradshaw, still holding hands, began to drift away from the burning ship, with Bradshaw offering continuous encouragement to the injured Giacchi, urging him to stay awake. They spotted the shapes of smaller boats coming and going, which they assumed to be E-boats still in the area. As they moved further and further away from LST-507, the sounds made by the other men in the water abated and although Giacchi and Bradshaw could see other groups of survivors clinging to a couple of life rafts and pieces of wreckage, they decided to keep their distance and stick together.

Having drifted in the freezing water for over four hours, they saw a light 'in the distance', which they both privately assumed must be their imaginations playing tricks on them. However, they both soon realised that they could not possibly be imagining the exact same thing at the same time. They had no idea whether the light signified the approach of a friendly or an enemy vessel, but decided that either way, they did not really care. If it meant they could get out of the freezing water, any rescue was welcome. It seemed to Giacchi that everything then happened at once, as a British corvette approached alongside them, her crew lowering ropes to help the struggling men on board. Bradshaw helped Giacchi up first, as the latter was wounded and now so weak, then Bradshaw followed himself.

Once on board, Giacchi recalls being struck by the opulence of the interior of the ship and the portraits of the Royal Family, which hung from the walls of the wardroom. Both men were given a shot of whisky and some dry clothes, while Giacchi's wounds were attended to. Later, as they headed inland, Giacchi heard a strange knocking sound against the bow of the ship and realised that this was the hull of the corvette striking against the dead bodies in the water. Turning to one of the British sailors, Giacchi looked at him questioningly and was told with an air of apology that there was no way of avoiding this.

Arriving on dry land, Giacchi and his comrades were warned to speak to no-one about what had occurred. Later, like Angelo Crapanzano, Patsy Giacchi was ordered to participate in the D-Day landings, even though he had assumed he might be given a period of leave to recover from what had happened.

According to his own recollection of events, Lieutenant Eugene Eckstam, medical officer on board LST-507, had decided against jumping from LST-507 into the water and had instead climbed down the cargo nets, lowering himself more gently into the water. Unlike many of the US Navy men, who were wearing kapok life jackets, Eckstam recalls that he had been issued with an inflatable life belt, like that worn by Patsy Giacchi and, like Giacchi, he knew how to use it. He inflated the belt and allowed it to rise up to his armpits before releasing himself from the cargo net. Almost immediately, he noticed many soldiers in the water who had not done the same. With their belts inflated around their waists and, in some cases, wearing their full packs on their backs, they had toppled forwards 'heads in the water and feet in the air'. By Eckstam's account, the army men had never received proper training in how to use a life belt.

Eckstam's recollections of his time in the water seem hazy and he simply states that he remained there for 'over two hours, fully dressed and insulated', making no mention of seeing any dead or wounded during this time. This may be because he does not wish to recall those sights, or it could be that his medical training had inured him to such visions—at least to a greater extent, perhaps, than some of the other men, who found it all more shocking.

As to his eventual rescue by LST-*515*, Eckstam remembers putting his knee on a boat ramp and then climbing up a Jacob's ladder. Half way through this process, he recalls having a sense of 'awakening', which implies that he had, perhaps, switched off mentally during his time in the water and, in that way was able to survive the freezing conditions and traumatic surroundings.

The LST docked at Portland, where the survivors were taken off and given dry clothing by the American Red Cross before being taken to an army field hospital at Sherborne. Eckstam also participated in the Normandy landings, being reassigned to LST-*391*, although he describes the events of 6 June at Utah Beach as a 'piece of cake' when compared to what happened to him on the night of 28 April off the Devon coast.

Ed Panter, who recalled 'jumping off the stern' of LST-*507* in the company of Eugene Eckstam and 'swimming away from the ship' also remembers noticing almost immediately, that Eckstam had brought his gas mask and was carrying it with him. Panter says he told his fellow medic to get rid of the gas mask and that the two of them swam together to a life raft, which was 'surrounded by [up] to 100 members of our crew'. Before too long, the extreme cold of the water, coupled with shock, began to take their toll on Panter and he lost the feeing in his hands and legs.

Panter's next recollection is of actually being on board LST-*515* and he makes no mention of his actual rescue or how this came about. He was suffering from hypothermia, but after his wet clothing was removed and he was given brandy and coffee, he began to feel better and moved around the ship, checking to see who else had survived.

Once on land, Panter was reunited with his wallet—the only possession he retained from the ship—and then he and his friends made their way to a Red Cross building, via a short stop at a public house where Panter bought everyone a whisky with the money he had in his wallet. On arrival at the Red Cross building, they were issued with more clothing. Like so many other survivors, Panter also participated in the D-Day landings.

Petty Officer Steve Sadlon, in common with a lot of other men, recalls that he began screaming out for help almost as soon as he hit the water. Having jumped off LST-507, he managed to swim through the flames and dead bodies that surrounded the ship, until he reached calmer waters. A nearby officer told him that there was no point in crying out for help as none would be coming, so Sadlon stopped screaming, quietened down and focused on staying alive. Like Eckstam and the army men, Sadlon was wearing an inflatable life belt which, fortunately, had settled under his arms. In this way, when hypothermia began to take its toll—which it did—and Sadlon blacked out, his head was kept clear of the water. His next recollection is of being on board one of the LSTs, having been rescued. He was later informed that the LST had actually been gathering in dead bodies, of which it had been assumed that Sadlon was one, when the crew had noticed that he was 'foaming at the mouth', so the medics on board the ship had started to work on resuscitating him.

Once on shore, Sadlon was taken to a US military hospital, where he recalls his treatment as being 'rough', feeling that the survivors were 'considered dogs', because the medical staff had been told to behave as though they were veterinarians, rather than doctors. Having been discharged from the hospital, Sadlon and a few of his fellow survivors were sent to Plymouth, where they were kept busy unloading ammunition from ships in the harbour. They were made to work at night and were kept separate from the other men, it having been impressed upon them that they must say nothing about their experiences during Exercise Tiger.

Shortly before the Normandy landings, Sadlon was reassigned to LST-500 and, like Eckstam, he found the invasion onto Utah Beach to be a 'walk in the park' when compared to his experiences at Slapton Sands.

The men who abandoned LST-531 faced similar problems to those encountered by the men who had left LST-507; the main difference being the lack of time afforded to the survivors of 531, as their ship was sinking so quickly.

Ensign Douglas Harlander, having given the order to abandon ship, which few others heard in the panic, found himself in the freezing waters of the English Channel and knew that he must get away from the rapidly sinking ship as quickly as possible. Kicking off his one remaining shoe—the other having been lost when he jumped overboard—Harlander began to swim through the burning gasoline and oil that covered the surface of the water. Before long, he reached a life raft, which already had around fifteen men clinging to its sides and he joined them.

As the hours progressed, Harlander became weaker and weaker, as did the other men around the raft who, one by one, slipped off and drowned. Dawn approached and eventually, Harlander was picked up by the British destroyer, HMS *Onslow*, whose crew lowered a line, which Harlander was just about able to tie under his arms, so they could lift him aboard. It was only then that he learned that he was the only man to survive from that life raft, the others having drowned or succumbed to hypothermia, while waiting for help to arrive.

HMS *Onslow* headed for Portsmouth, where Harlander disembarked, together with the few other survivors that the destroyer had collected, wearing borrowed Royal Navy uniform. He was taken to a US Army hospital and was discharged the following day, whereupon, as the most senior surviving officer of LST-531, he was driven to Plymouth to make his report to Rear-Admiral Moon.

Having got himself up on to the deck of LST-531, John A. Brown had climbed into a life raft, where he had helped other men to get on board. In his letter to Lieutenant John Hill's sister Marion Irving, Brown recalls that there were about 'twenty-six men with the raft', one of whom was an officer of the small boat crew. They paddled quickly away from the stricken LST-531 and then drifted in the water for 'about six hours', until they were rescued by a 'British boat'. On board this vessel, they were all given immediate medical treatment for shock and slight wounds, while the ship made its way back to Plymouth, where Brown was issued with dry clothing and then reassigned to a new ship.

Ensign Raymond Gosselin had managed to jump clear of LST-531, in spite of having a broken leg and 'a few minor wounds'. He waited in the water until after the ship had gone down and the sea was calmer, before swimming—with some difficulty—to a life raft, where he found 'other men there already'. These men moved around in their life raft, picking up other survivors, although there were not many to be found. In his letter to Lieutenant Hill's wife, Florence, Gosselin describes seeing another naval man, Eugene Hock, on a separate life raft, doing the same thing. Both men were wounded and Hock was sent back to America, while Gosselin remained in England, recuperating from his injuries.

Although we do not know which LST John Maltese was on, he gives a description of the aftermath, saying that the 'sea was red' with the blood of the dead men. He also comments that even the following day, the water was still burning.

John Cullen, the second coxswain aboard His Majesty's Rescue Motor Launch 532 did not have to wait long to receive the order to return to Portland. The commanding officer of HMS *Attack* decided that the risk to the rescue boats from the wild firing of the LSTs was too great, and ordered the six motor launches to withdraw from the area. Cullen knew that to remain in the vicinity would in all probably have turned them from 'saviours into victims' as they would very likely have come under 'friendly fire' and, with the fuel tanks of an RML being on deck, this would have been catastrophic, but nonetheless, he still harboured feelings of 'bitter disappointment' as they turned away from the scene of the burning ships and headed back to port. He knew that each boat had the capacity to take on around fifty survivors, so that they could, between the six of them, have saved somewhere in the region of three hundred men.

Meanwhile, back in England, the military hospitals and bases had to be made ready to receive the wounded. One of the doctors serving at the 228th Station Hospital in Sherborne, Dorset was Captain Ralph Greene of the US Army Medical Corps and in the normal course of events most of his time was spent dealing with routine medical cases. In the early hours of 28 April, however, he received a telephone call from the adjutant, telling him to get all the officers together in the recreation room immediately, where they were addressed by Colonel James Kendall, commander of the hospital.

He explained to the group of medics that they would be receiving 'hundreds of emergency cases of shock due to immersion, compounded by explosion wounds'. He went on to tell the doctors and nurses gathered before him that, in an unusual request, SHAEF had demanded that the medics should behave as though they were 'veterinarians'. They were to 'ask no questions and take no histories'. Like the men who had participated directly in the exercise, they were told to say nothing about what was happening and were warned that anyone who did speak out, would be 'subject to court-martial'. Everyone was confined to the base for the time being as they awaited the incoming wounded, who arrived in a 'stream of ambulances'.

Over the next few hours, the doctors and nurses worked on the men who arrived 'cold, wet and many in great pain', but with the exception of the medics talking to each other, there was no speech at all. Most of the men responded well to treatment and could be returned to their units, although some died, but at no time was any explanation given and within a few days, all of the participants of the exercise had left the hospital.

This account helps to explain why Steve Sadlon might have felt so badly treated by the medical staff upon his arrival at hospital—since it was to the 228th Station Hospital that he was sent. The medics there cannot be held responsible for having to behave the way they did: they were acting under orders and, according to Greene, were as confused and upset as the men they were treating.

Back in Devon, young John Spooner, who had enjoyed his first Saturday helping out at the US base at Heathfield, near his home in Teignmouth, woke early again the following weekend, got himself ready and cycled to the base. The previous weekend, just as he was leaving at the end of the day, he had heard the men being told that they would be moving to Dartmouth to take part in an exercise codenamed 'Tiger', but John was told by Sergeant McKinnon to report for duty as usual, as the Americans would be back from their exercises by the Saturday. He was stunned, upon his arrival at the base, to find it deserted, except for a guard who was standing by the gate. On discovering who John was, the guard handed him a five dollar bill, with Sergeant McKinnon's compliments, for the work he had done the previous week. The guard seemed upset, so John left and rode home slowly, only learning much later of what had happened in Exercise Tiger. He never spent or exchanged the five dollar bill, but kept it in remembrance of those who had died many of whom were friends he had briefly made.

CHAPTER SEVEN

'It Could Happen to You'

The recovery of bodies and controversy over burials

The men who managed to jump from the burning and sinking LSTs, who survived the flaming waters and freezing seas and later spoke of their ordeals, told of seeing bodies in various states. Some were burned, some dismembered, others drowned, or there were those men who, others recalled, exhausted from trying to stay alive, simply drifted away and disappeared beneath the surface of the icy English Channel. In addition to these men, who were painfully visible to their surviving comrades, were those who failed to make it off of the sinking ships. These included the men who burned to death on LST-507, as described by Lieutenant Eugene Eckstam, or men like Patty Moreno, who did not follow his friend Patsy Giacchi up onto the deck and, therefore, had no time to escape when the torpedo struck the ship. These men either burned or drowned and, in either case, went down with their ship, it becoming their unmarked, watery grave. For those whose job it was to recover the visible bodies, a gruesome and lengthy task lay ahead.

Aboard His Majesty's Rescue Motor Launch 532, Second Coxswain John Cullen and his fellow crew members had been ordered back to Portland, together with the other five launches, in the wake of some random firing by the LSTs and had arrived there at approximately 04.30. However, they did not have to wait long for their new orders, as it was decided almost immediately, that they should head back to the site of the E-boat attack at first light, once they could be sure that the gunners on board the LSTs would no longer be able to mistake the motor launches for enemy craft.

The men had a speedy breakfast and headed back out to sea just after 05.00, arriving at the scene at around daybreak where, in Cullen's words, they found 'debris spread over a very large area', in the centre of which was one of the pontoons which had been ditched by LST-58 as she made her escape from the E-boats. Commander Scott of HMRML 532 decided that the pontoon ought to be towed back to Portland as, left where it was, it presented a 'navigational hazard'.

Together with the First Officer, Lieutenant Marryott, Cullen launched a dinghy and the two men made their way towards the pontoon so they could attach a tow rope. However, once this was done and HMRML 532 revved up her engines and attempted to take the strain, the pontoon would not budge. Unbeknownst to Marryott and Cullen in the dinghy, the pontoon had become 'firmly secured' to one of the sunken LSTs. Glancing over the side of the dinghy to try to see what was wrong, Cullen saw, for the first time, that the propellers of the motor launch had churned up several bodies that had not been visible during their approach.

Commander Scott did not want to take his vessel in among the bodies for fear that they might become further caught up in the propellers, so he told Cullen and Marryott to return to the motor launch, which they did. Scott then asked Cullen to get into the water to fetch in the bodies by hand.

The sea was still cold and Cullen had to work quickly, spending one and a half hours gathering in bodies and bringing them back to the motor launch for them to be winched on board. Some were dismembered, others were caught up in cargo netting, so that Cullen had to swim under the water to cut them free. Only when the Captain was satisfied that all of the visible bodies had been removed from the water, did he help Cullen back aboard HMRML 532. He was, by now, 'close to exhaustion' and was covered with blankets, but found that he still 'could not stop shivering'.

In his account of that morning, Cullen recalls that in that moment, there was 'absolute silence': the engines of the motor launch were stopped; no-one spoke and 'even the sea birds were quiet'. He says that it 'felt as if the world was paying reverence to the brave dead men that were lying on the deck'.

The motor launch headed back towards Portland and while *en route*, Cullen went below deck to change into his Number One uniform, so that he could pipe each of the dead men ashore, once the boat had docked. Arriving back in Portland at approximately 11.00, they were met by American trucks that were waiting to collect the bodies. Cullen duly piped each body ashore, watched over by the commanding officer of HMS *Attack*, Captain J. P. Farquharson.

Once the trucks had departed, Cullen and the rest of the crew of the motor launch had their lunch before being addressed by their captain, who told them that they must not tell anyone about what had happened and what they had seen and done. The reasons he gave were that, if rumours got around, then the plans for the invasion might become known to the Germans and also that such a heavy loss of life would undermine morale. The next day, HMRML 532 sailed back through Lyme Bay *en route* to Dartmouth and Cullen saw that ships were sweeping the area, looking for more bodies.

LST-515, having returned to the scene of the E-boat attack at around 05.00, picked up many survivors, not all of whom managed to remain alive for very long once they had been rescued. One of the men aboard LST-515 was Quartermaster Eugene Carney, who served with the 4th Infantry Division. He recalls that, after rescuing so many who were still alive, the number of dead bodies on board the ship sadly continued to mount as they gave up the fight for life. One of Carney's daunting tasks was to move the dead onto stretchers, so they could be carried to the lower decks. He was joined in this by some of the younger sailors and they found the job even more onerous than Carney, as they had never had to handle a dead body before. Carney, on the other hand, had more experience in such matters, as his uncle, back in the US, owned a funeral home, so Carney was used to being around the dead. However, as the night progressed, even the younger men grew more used to their job, which continued into the morning.

A warrant officer on board HMS *Obedient*, arriving at the scene of the attack in the early hours of the morning, described the sight that greeted him and his shipmates as 'appalling'. In his account of events, he recalls seeing 'hundreds of bodies' of American soldiers and sailors in the water, some of whom had limbs missing. He saw a small landing craft, which had been lowered by an LST [presumably LST-515], moving around the water, with her ramps down 'literally scooping up bodies, driving them ashore and dumping them on the beaches'. The crew of the *Obedient* herself gathered in many bodies and according to the warrant officer, also nine survivors, although separate reports indicate that there was only one survivor picked up by this ship. Other vessels also arrived to help search for survivors, but there were none left by this stage, so they ended up collecting in the dead. The bodies were either handed over to US ships, or taken ashore and given to the US Army to be loaded into waiting trucks.

Regardless of how, or by whom, the men were collected from the water, their bodies were loaded into ambulances or trucks and were driven to Brookwood Cemetery in Surrey, where they were buried and wooden crosses were erected showing each man's name, his rank, the ship on which he had served and the date of his death, which was always given as 28 April 1944. For the time being, these graves were intended to be temporary, as it was assumed that once hostilities had ceased, some of the families would want the bodies of their loved ones repatriated to the US.

In a letter to Lieutenant John Hill's sister, Marion Irving, John Brown describes a visit which he made to Brookwood Cemetery in May 1945, describing it accurately as a 'British burial ground with the Americans taking over a plot near the edge'. This section of the cemetery was situated in a plot which is now behind the American Battle Monuments Commission Chapel, beyond a fence, where there was a large field, big enough to hold the casualties in one plot, but which also contained some American casualties from the First World War. Brown took photographs of this part of the cemetery as a whole and several of the individual grave markers in particular, which he sent to Mrs Irving. There is absolutely no doubt that the men who died on the night of 28 April 1944 on convoy T-4 were buried, albeit temporarily, at Brookwood Cemetery.

Despite this, the whereabouts of the bodies of the men who perished has since become a matter of conjecture, fuelled by the stories of one particular local woman and the need of others to find conspiracy theories at every turn.

In November 1984, a service was held at Slapton Village Church to dedicate a tank, raised from the sea bed, in memory of the men who had died in Exercise Tiger. This tank had been salvaged by local guesthouse owner, Ken Small, in an act which had taken some ten years or more to accomplish. There was a great deal of local publicity surrounding both the raising of the tank and the dedication. As well as investing time and money in the raising of the tank, Small had also begun a campaign to erect a permanent memorial to the dead of Exercise Tiger and found himself being interviewed regularly by television, radio and newspaper journalists.

At around the same time, a woman who had lived in the village of Stoke Fleming during the war, named Dorothy Seekings, came forward to the now gathering media, with a story of having witnessed a 'mass burial' in a field just outside Blackawton in the spring of 1944. She maintained that, at the time, she had been given a ride in a US Army truck, which had been transporting 'wet' bodies, stating that, when the truck had stopped by the field, the driver had climbed down, opened the back of the vehicle and invited her to look at the bodies lying inside. She said that the mens' uniforms were wet, as though they had been in the water and claimed that these bodies had never since been removed from their mass grave, implying by this statement that they still lie there today.

Months later, in another interview, Mrs Seekings embellished this original story, now claiming that there had been more than one truck full of dead bodies and that, in a second incident, one of the vehicles had pulled up outside her father's bakery, a few days after she had first witnessed the burial of the dead American soldiers. Again, the driver had evidently dismounted and had revealed to her the contents of his vehicle, which contained yet more dead bodies, still evidently wet. Now, in this second account, instead of one mass grave, Mrs Seekings was able to describe several of them, each in a separate location around the area, although she did admit that she had not actually witnessed any further burials herself. She added that the bodies concerned had washed up on Blackpool Sands, just up the coast from Slapton.

People began to take an interest in Mrs Seekings' suggestions, including the families of the victims of the E-boat attack, who were now becoming more aware of the events that had taken place forty years earlier. They began to wonder how America could have treated her dead so shabbily.

Like many others, Ken Small had heard Mrs Seekings' accounts of the mass burials and he began to wonder whether they might, in fact, be true. He started to make enquiries about the possibilities of there being bodies still buried somewhere in the South Hams. Working on the premise of the dead having been washed ashore, Small investigated further into Mrs Seekings' suggestions and found that other locals also told similar stories, but that they offered alternative versions, most particularly as to where and how the bodies were buried. Small was informed that the US military had constructed concrete bunkers, placed the dead inside and then either blown them up, or blocked them up, thereby sealing in the bodies. With information such as this, it seemed as though the stories of mass graves in farmers' fields might actually be true.

However, by late 1985, Small had received definite confirmation from the American authorities that all bodies from convoy T-4 were taken by ship to Portland, more than thirty miles from Slapton and Blackpool Sands. At this stage, faced with irrefutable evidence, he began to distance himself from the claims surrounding mass graves and unofficial burial sites in Devon.

Nonetheless, Mrs Seekings persisted with her stories, despite the fact that everyone whom she offered as a potential corroborative witness could not or would not confirm her side of the story. In the meantime, she appeared on television and radio throughout the world, revealing the details of her tale. It should also be noted that, until the event began to gain more notice in Devon, with the raising of the tank, Mrs Seekings had said nothing to the authorities or any of the media about her experiences in the spring of 1944.

One has to point out that some locals maintain that in the fields where Mrs Seekings claims the burials took place, there are patches or areas where the crops grow better and greener than elsewhere within the same fields. Despite this, the farmers who own these fields, some of whom have farmed their land all their lives and for many generations, state that they have ploughed and dug the fields in question for years on end, without finding a single shred of evidence that anyone or anything is buried there.

It remains clear that some of these stories are fuelled by a lack of official information having been made available by the US authorities. In the immediate aftermath of Exercise Tiger, the element of secrecy was an absolute imperative, hence all the survivors and those who came into contact with them, were warned—usually on threat of a court martial—to say nothing about what had happened. The immediate reason for the demand for secrecy was obvious. The Normandy landings were only weeks away and no-one wanted the Germans to know what was about to take place, or give them the opportunity of guessing where the invasion might happen.

This need for secrecy was made all the more important by the fact that ten of the officers on board the two LSTs that were sunk, had carried the status of BIGOT, meaning that they were privy to all of the details regarding the D-Day landings. (The name 'BIGOT' had been derived by reversing the wording 'TO GIB' which had been applied to all documents being sent to Gibraltar—the location of Eisenhower's headquarters—during Operation Torch in 1942. The status of BIGOT meant, simply, that the officer involved had been given access to some or all of the top-secret information relating to the D-Day landings and that his capture could endanger the operation). All ten of these officers were initially reported as missing after the E-boat attack and, until their bodies could be accounted for, the staff at SHAEF were at panic stations. Montgomery decided that answers must be had immediately and despatched his American Liaison Officer, Major Ralph Ingersoll to Devon to find out what had happened and ascertain the whereabouts of the bodies of the BIGOTs. Divers were sent down to the wrecks and extensive searches were made among the already recovered bodies, but for a while, it looked as though the plans for D-Day might have to be altered. However, Ingersoll was soon able to report that the bodies of all ten officers had been recovered, allaying the fear that they may have been captured by the Germans and could have been forced to reveal their knowledge of the Allied invasion plans. Nonetheless, secrecy remained paramount, at least until after D-Day. Despite this, reports of an attack by German E-boats in the English Channel did appear in various newspapers immediately afterwards, giving sketchy accounts and, throughout the summer, newspapers in England and America referred to the event. Indeed, a report appeared giving a few details of the attack in a Boston newspaper on 29 April, stating that 'Nazi motor torpedo boats attacked a destroyer-escorted British convoy on the English south coast yesterday, torpedoing a destroyer and sinking three of the convoyed vessels.' Although most of the details of this report are inaccurate, it is easy to see that the 'secrecy' element of Exercise Tiger was not strictly adhered to, even from day one and certainly not once the Normandy landings had taken place. As for the survivors who had been threatened with courts martial, while some men revealed the truth quite quickly after the event, many of them did not speak about their experiences until the mid-1980s, when more information began to come to light in several television documentaries.

Some of the men who held their silence for so long did so because of the initial orders they had received at the time from their commanding officers— they were told they must never speak of the event, so they did not. In other cases, men kept quiet because, in common with many survivors of war or trauma, they simply could not bring themselves to discuss it—especially with people who had not been there, and shared the same experiences: people who had no understanding of what had happened that night. If the survivors had met up, they might have talked, relayed their experiences and shared their stories, but the veterans of Exercise Tiger were scattered far and wide across America.

After the television documentaries were shown and the event gained more publicity in the mid to late 1980s, the survivors began to make contact with each other to discuss their mutual and shared memories. Some among them also began to carry out independent investigations into what had actually happened that night and, more specifically, how many of their comrades had died. These investigations led to some heady and interesting speculation over the number of casualties, some of which remains unresolved to this day.

The first casualty list, which was issued on 29 April 1944, the day after the attack, stated that the number of dead was 638, with 89 men wounded. After a few months, this figure was revised upwards, after a US Army historian examined the data and decided that the number of dead was 749, which has subsequently become the generally accepted figure. Since then, various interested parties, ranging from survivors of the event itself, to modern 'historians', have come forward with casualty figures which vary from 639, to well over 1,000, based on their different perspectives, mathematical equations and supposed 'evidence'. Some of these suggestions are extreme in number, a few verging on wild and point towards unsubstantiated conspiracy theories which might make for interesting reading, but for which there is little or no genuine corroboration, other than theory, supposition and wishful thinking.

One of the theories which has been put forward is that the number of personnel originally loaded onto the LSTs (and specifically LST-507) is in dispute. The reason for this is that LST-508, which should have sailed as part of convoy T-4, failed to do so because she had been damaged and that, therefore, her compliment of army 'passengers' was transferred, at the last minute, to LST-507. There is no documentary evidence for this having taken place, only the statements of a few survivors that the tank deck was packed with 'hundreds' of men—signifying presumably that there were more army men on board than the 282 attested to by Lieutenant James Murdock, the Executive Officer of LST-507. It must be said that Murdock's official account was given within weeks of the exercise, while the other survivors' memories were recalled many years afterwards. In addition, the term 'hundreds' is really quite subjective and cannot be taken as a factual recognition that LST-507 was definitely overloaded or 'double' loaded, as some have claimed. On the other hand, there are modern historians who claim that Lieutenant Murdock was told by senior officers to falsify his statement and to say that 282 was the number of army personnel on board, when the genuine figure had really been higher than this. However, one must question what would be the purpose in doing this? After all, hundreds of men had died, what would be the harm in admitting to a few hundred more and what would be the point in attempting to hide or disguise the involvement of additional troops? Added to this, of the units that were due to travel on LST-508 (which included the 4th Quartermaster Company and the 8th and 22nd Regiments of the 4th Infantry Division), no-one has come forward to say they were on LST-507 and none of the men from these units are listed among the dead or known survivors. It seems more than a little strange that these units only should escape without a single casualty, when others were so badly hit.

Lieutenant Eugene Eckstam, the medical officer on board LST-507, made it his mission, following his retirement from the medical profession, to research everything he possibly could about Exercise Tiger. He tracked down survivors, trawled through boxes of letters, statements, articles and official documents trying to piece together an accurate picture of what had occurred that night. As a result of his extensive researches, he arrived at the casualty figure of 639 dead, maintaining that other numbers were based on 'estimates'. According to Eckstam, Eisenhower released a bulletin on 8 August 1944, explaining the events surrounding Exercise Tiger and revealing that two LSTs had been sunk and one damaged. Army casualties were quoted in this statement as 441 and Navy dead as 198, making a total of 639. As already stated, there seems little point in the military lying about these figures: if there were a few hundred more, why not just say so? To the families of the dead, each and every casualty was tragic; 639 deaths meant that many families would have been in mourning, but in wartime, what would be the need to massage these figures? If the number of dead had been 700 or 800, or more, those families would still grieve for them. The nature of their deaths, while not perhaps something to shout about from a military perspective, did not diminish their lives, their contribution or their sacrifices and America is not a country to defame its war dead.

Eckstam explains that the figure of 639 had, to his knowledge, first been mentioned by Eisenhower in a radio despatch of 13 May 1944, but we also know that this was the number officially announced on 29 April. Furthermore Eckstam states that the executive officer on each ship was obliged to know the number of personnel on board and that, if Murdock attested to there having been 282, then that would have been the information which he was given on the unit roster by the senior army officer on board LST-507, Captain Seifert. There is no way of verifying this figure, as much of the paperwork went down with the ship, but other than a mysterious and, frankly, unnecessary conspiracy by senior officers, there would be no need to lie about any of it.

With regard to the now generally accepted casualty total of 749, Eckstam disputes this, maintaining in his correspondence that this cannot necessarily be corroborated. He quotes from a 'cable' sent by Rear-Admiral Moon on 28 August 1944 at 14.08 to all Task Force Commanders in the area, copying in SHAEF, as follows:

> Regret to report LSTs 507, 531 loaded with estimated 744 Army and 282 Navy Personnel sunk by torpedoes. Total known ambulatory survivors, 257, litter cases 33. LST 289 received following damage, wrecked steering gear and crew's quarters. Crack appearing amidships. 4 of crew dead, 9 missing, 18 wounded, 1 critically. 4 Army personnel wounded. LST towed to Dartmouth.

As Eckstam is keen to point out, the figures given by Moon are estimates only, but add up in this way:

> 744 Army + 282 Navy = 1026 total personnel on board LSTs 507 and 531.
> 257 + 33 = 290 known survivors from LSTs 507 and 531.
> 13 confirmed dead or missing from LST 289.

If one subtracts the known survivor total of 290 (LSTs 507 and 531) from the estimated number of personnel on board both of these two vessels (1,026), one is left with a total of 736 dead, then one adds the thirteen dead or missing men from LST-289 to arrive at a total of 749.

However, according to Eckstam, this figure should not be treated as accurate or conclusive, because in Moon's cable, the number of personnel on board the two ships is clearly estimated and, therefore, the whole equation that follows is questionable.

It is, of course, possible that the total of 749 includes the men who perished in the 'friendly fire' incident which took place on the beach on the morning of 27 April. It might be argued that these deaths may have been 'hushed up' and included within the casualty listings for the E-boat attack, due to the way in which they occurred. However, there remains no evidence in support of this argument, so it cannot be verified one way or the other, regardless of whether the figures have been secretly 'massaged', or openly amended. Whatever happened, over the years, the total number of casualties of 749 has become generally accepted and quoted, except that is, by those who believe the figure to be considerably higher.

Among such believers is Dale Rodman, another survivor from LST-507, who served with the 33rd Chemical Decontamination Company. Having got off of the ship, he was, he claims picked up by HMS *Azalea* on the morning of 28 April. In correspondence with Eugene Eckstam, Rodman maintains that Eckstam's evidence is at fault and that the genuine casualty figure was much higher than the 639 which Eckstam believed, or even the 749 which he also discussed.

Rodman asserts his belief that LST-507 should have been loaded with 352 Army personnel and 161 Naval crew, making a total of 513, while LST-531 should have contained 392 men from various Army units and 121 from the Navy, also (curiously) adding up to 513. He maintains that LST-507 was, in reality, 'double loaded' (even though Eckstam, Patsy Giacchi and Angelo Crapanzano were also aboard that vessel and make no mention of this). Rodman states that 70 of the 352 Army men due to be loaded on LST-507 were taken off (so, 352 − 70 = 282 which is the number which Lieutenant Murdock maintained were on board), then Rodman states that 294 additional men were brought in from LST-508. He believes that Captain Seifert's documents were accurate: the 282 Army men on board LST-507 were the men actually under his own command as the senior army officer assigned to that vessel. The men who had transferred from LST-508 were, however, not his responsibility: that duty lay with the Senior Army Officer from LST-508. Rodman claims that Rear Admiral Moon would not have mentioned the double loading in his 'cable' giving estimated casualty and survivor numbers, because he would not have known about it. Nonetheless, it seems curious that, throughout his account of events, Lieutenant Murdock maintains that the number of Army personnel loaded on LST-507 was 282 and makes no mention of transfers from other vessels. Again, the question remains: Why would Murdock lie about this?

In his correspondence, Rodman goes on to use several mathematical equations, all based around the 'double loaded' figures that he has presented, to arrive at a different number of casualties. He is forced, however, to admit that he has no accurate knowledge of the number of dead, but puts forward several arguments and different proposals for totals, which grow each time from 1,040 to 1,167, to 1,398 and then 1,404. The 'evidence' for these arguments and totals ranges from the number of trucks it would have taken to transport the bodies (making the uncorroborated assumption that all of the trucks would be full), to the amount of time it would take to embalm the corpses.

Rodman points out in his correspondence that this is not the only falsehood of which he believes the military and government to be guilty. Not only does he state that he believes that the casualty figures were falsified (for whatever reason), but that also the number of sunk and damaged LSTs were disguised. His basis for this argument commences with his assertion that, despite the fact that the official logs of HMS *Azalea* reported that she picked up no survivors,

he himself had been rescued by that vessel 'along with many others'. Prior
to this, he says, he was aboard an LCVP (Landing Craft Vehicle/Personnel),
which contained thirty-nine other men. Much later, in 1995, it would seem
that another survivor, William Gould, had related to Rodman that he had
been on an LCVP with 70 men and had been rescued by a British corvette, so
Rodman estimated the number of survivors on the corvette, which he took
to be HMS *Azalea*, to be 110. Another man, named Vincent Rolleri from
the same company as Rodman, had also recounted being aboard an LCVP
with roughly forty men. Rodman discovered five men in total (six, including
himself) who had been picked up by 'different ships', as follows:

D. Rodman—HMS *Azalea*
V. Rolleri—Unidentified US ship
E. Polovitch—LST-515
S. Stout—Unidentified British destroyer
W. Gould—Unidentified British corvette
J. Siezmore [*sic*]—Unidentified British destroyer

Rodman argues that 'Since [these men] were rescued by different ships, they
could not be from the same LST' and according to his reckoning, this would
'make 6 the number of LST sunk or damaged during Exercise Tiger.' However,
the official listing of known survivors shows that at least four of these six men
came from LST-507, which rather rules out Rodman's suggestions.

Equally, John Maltese of the 462nd Amphibious Truck Company states in
his account of the event that there were 752 casualties, all of whom were
buried in England. He comments that no-one was allowed to talk about or
write home giving details regarding anything that had happened and that men
who did were court-martialled and says that the families of the men who died
were not told about their deaths 'until years later'. He finally points out that
Rear-Admiral Moon 'committed suicide the following day' after the attack.

These stories, like so many others, might seem attractive to those who
want to find conspiracies and smoke-screens in every aspect of the exercise,
turning the whole event into something, perhaps, a little more exciting and
newsworthy, but they are really based on suppositions, hearsay and dubious
memory, rather than fact. There are those who have used accounts such as
the ones provided by Dale Rodman and John Maltese to demonstrate the
supposed 'reality' of the event, but one man's fact, taken in isolation, cannot
be taken as the whole truth, without something concrete to back it up.

It is now virtually impossible to say exactly how many men lost their lives
in the E-boat attack, which must be treated as a separate event to the friendly
fire incident of the previous day. However, for the sake of being as accurate

as is feasible—from a distance of nearly seventy years—it has been possible to assess the list of casualties provided by the American Battle Monuments Commission. The UK-based charity, Exercise Tiger Trust have undertaken to individually check and cross-reference each of these casualties on a name-by-name basis, to ascertain each man's full military record, including his date of death and place of burial or commemoration. By compiling all of this analysis, which has taken over four months of painstaking research to accumulate, the number of known and confirmed named casualties arrived at is 637. It is unlikely that there were fewer casualties, but no-one can say with any degree of certainty that this figure is entirely true and accurate. All that can be said is that, without any further, proper, corroborated evidence, this figure is the best one to hand at the moment.

The continued and contentious debate over the number of casualties involved might raise the profile of those involved but it does little else, other than detract from what matters most: the casualties themselves, whose sacrifices were eclipsed by those made in the event for which they were rehearsing, some forty days later. To the survivors fell the secrecy, but also the guilt that often follows such traumatic events. Their feelings about that night and their fallen comrades may be summed up in the words of John A. Brown, in a letter written to Lieutenant John Hill's sister, Marion Irving, dated 17 February 1945. In this letter, Brown describes his first meeting with Lieutenant Hill and says that he 'was not an officer at heart and was only there to do the duties that he had been assigned to do'. Going on to explain their future relationship, Brown explains that he 'greatly admired' Hill and, following his death in the sinking of LST-531, wrote of this officer: 'The others of the crew have paid the highest price for freedom while I am still serving my time the best that I can. For them I admire and respect but there is one that I would have given anything to have helped to save. Of the entire group I miss him the most. The medals that his wife has received are only a token in memory of him. May they be cherished. This letter can only tell to a small degree the loss that he caused. His loss could equally be missed by the Navy as he is at home … give my love to his son. I only hope he is as good as his Dad. The sorrow that his death has caused should be takened [*sic*] as his gift to the US. That I am sure would be his wish.'

CHAPTER EIGHT

'We Must All Stick Together'

Investigations into Exercise Tiger and reports of different personnel

Looking at the accounts of the individual survivors, it quickly becomes clear that they all believe that someone, somewhere must be to blame for the events that took place in Lyme Bay in the early hours of 28 April 1944. It is a firmly held opinion that a tragedy such as this cannot have happened out of the blue, for no reason and most argue that at some level, someone in authority must have made a calamitous and costly error.

The US Navy and Army survivors of Convoy T-4 point the finger at several different aspects. Generally speaking, for some, the obvious scapegoat was the Royal Navy, who not only failed to supply an adequate escort for the convoy, but who then compounded this felony by taking such a long time to react or provide any kind of support, once the attack was under way, leaving the men on board the LSTs feeling like sitting ducks. Others are more broad in their finger pointing, blaming the senior officers of both Allied armies and navies— essentially everyone from Eisenhower downwards, who had any involvement in the planning or the execution of the exercise.

With regard to specifics, a lot of the survivors are quick to recall the lack of training they received in the correct employment of inflatable life belts. Those who managed to jump overboard from the burning, sinking LSTs, remember the sight of their comrades upturned in the water, their faces beneath the waves and their feet in the air, because their life belts were worn incorrectly. While some, such as Patsy Giacchi, maintained that adequate training was given to his group, this would seem not to have applied to every unit involved in the exercise, as many claim to have been told nothing. Even for those who were trained in how to use a life belt, there remains another cause for complaint within this area of the exercise, namely that they had not been drilled in how to react in emergencies on board the ships. Most of the naval crew men had done this during their training, either in the United States, during their trans-Atlantic crossing, or while in Great

Britain, but for almost all of the army personnel, the idea of an attack at sea and the knowledge of how to react in such circumstances, were completely alien. In his account of the night, Patsy Giacchi recalls the panic of one man from his own unit who had gone up on deck, but had left his own life belt below decks. Just as Giacchi and his friend Bradshaw were about to jump off the ship, the man had grabbed Giacchi and tried to take his life belt from him. Bradshaw had pushed the man away and he and Giacchi had jumped into the sea. The man, who Giacchi named in his account, perished with the ship, although his body was recovered, unlike so many others, and he is buried at Cambridge Military Cemetery. In Giacchi's eyes, this behaviour reinforces his opinion that, while the men in his unit might have been taught how to use their life belts, they were ill-prepared to face a real 'abandon ship' situation and many of them panicked.

From an overall military perspective, the requirement to look at what had happened—and more particularly what had gone wrong—was imperative. With D-Day only weeks away it was important that any lessons that could be learned were quickly acted upon. At the same time, however, the close proximity of D-Day also made the investigations difficult: everyone was simply too busy focusing on the job in hand to be concerned with the disaster behind them. Not only that, but the Fabius exercises were either still on-going or imminent, as some of them had started before Exercise Tiger and they would continue into May and several of the personnel involved in Exercise Tiger were also involved in the planning for Exercise Fabius, as well as Operation Overlord. These men were, therefore, already stretched to breaking point, without the additional requirement to attend interviews and complete reports on the events surrounding the Exercise Tiger E-boat attack. Nonetheless, investigations and enquiries had to be carried out, not only to understand what had gone wrong and to ensure that it could not go wrong again, but also in case it turned out that there was something or—more importantly—someone that needed to be changed or replaced before the rehearsal became the reality. In order to carry out the enquiries satisfactorily, it was necessary to look at the actions of the officers involved at the time.

The first indication that many senior commanders had of the incident had come when Convoy T-4 had failed to arrive at Slapton Sands at the designated time on the morning of 28 April. General Omar Bradley, Commander of US Army Forces in North-West Europe, was displeased by this delay, but had to wait until the afternoon of that day to be given an explanation. Upon hearing of the attack, his initial enquiries regarding the number of casualties met with a noncommittal response, leaving him to question why the whole convoy had failed to arrive as expected.

Meanwhile, Rear-Admiral Moon, Naval Commander of Force 'U' and the officer in charge of Exercise Tiger, was aboard USS *Bayfield* and was told of the E-boat attack some five hours after it had taken place. His immediate reaction was to send off his Chief of Staff, Captain Tompkins to the scene with three escort vessels to help in the search for survivors and retrieval of the dead. Moon also requested air support and search facilities from the RAF and sent word to all ports to make ready to receive the wounded and survivors. He then returned to directing the remainder of the exercise.

Later that evening, Eisenhower was informed of the tragedy and was told that casualties were more severe than had first been thought and that the sinking of two LSTs and damage to a third would give the United States Navy some serious planning and logistical problems in the build-up to D-Day.

On the afternoon of 29 April, with Exercise Tiger completed, Rear-Admiral Moon reported to Rear-Admiral Alan Kirk, Commander of the Western Naval Task Force, to account for his actions. With Kirk were his Chief of Staff, Rear-Admiral Arthur Struble and the Commander of Landing Craft and Bases, Amphibious Forces (Europe), Rear-Admiral John Wilkes. In a meeting which took place aboard USS *Augusta*, Moon, who was accompanied by his Air and Assistant Plans Officer, Commander John Moreno, showed signs of great strain under questioning. Once this gathering was completed, it was followed by another at which Moon, still accompanied by Moreno, but now also joined by his Intelligence Officer, Commander Robert Thayer, interviewed the commanders of the various vessels involved in the exercise, including Lieutenant Shee from HMS *Scimitar* and Lieutenant-Commander Geddes from HMS *Azalea*. Both of the commanding officers from LSTs *507* and *531* had been killed in the attack, so they were represented by the senior surviving officers from those vessels: Lieutenant James Murdock (LST-*507*) and Ensign Douglas Harlander (LST-*531*).

Both Harlander and Geddes later reported that Moon demonstrated a great deal of tension during their interviews. While being questioned, Geddes admitted that HMS *Azalea* had received notification of the presence of E-boats at around midnight, but that the message was still being decoded when the attack began. The representatives from the US Navy questioned this, wondering why it would have taken two hours to decode a message, for which Geddes did not really have an answer. Geddes went on to point out that even if the message had been deciphered in time, there would have been little he could have done, because he could not communicate with the LSTs or any other American vessel, as the two navies were using different radio frequencies. Geddes was asked why this was and he said that he and Commander Bernard Skahill, the commodore of Convoy T-4, who had been on board LST-*515*, had been given the opportunity to get together prior to sailing to coordinate their radio frequencies, but that they had not done so, since no-one thought it important. Ultimately, this remarkable omission placed Geddes in a difficult position. During the exercise and attack, he was really accountable to his own senior officer, Rear-Admiral Sir Ralph Leatham, the British Naval Commander-in-Chief at Plymouth, not to Commander Skahill. However, in January 1944, before the exercises had begun, Leatham had agreed with Rear-Admiral John Hall, US Naval Commander of 'Force O', that all senior staff officers in the US Navy would be treated in exactly the same way as their British counterparts and that all information received by Leatham would be passed on to the Americans, together with recommendations for action. While the Americans had taken exception to the last part of this agreement, they welcomed the remainder. However, even once the presence of the E-boats became known at Plymouth, Leatham had been unable to communicate anything to Skahill because the British shore bases and ships were using different radio frequencies to those employed by the US Navy. So, while the Admiralty might well have been aware of there being E-boats in the area just after midnight on 28 April, the only sea-going vessel that could be informed of this was HMS *Azalea*. Despite Leatham's promise to Hall and the fact that Skahill was in charge of the convoy, neither Leatham nor Geddes could contact Skahill on LST-515, or Rear-Admiral Moon on USS *Bayfield*. Thus the convoy sailed on into danger, in blissful ignorance. As already said, therefore, Geddes was accountable to Leatham and, in some respects, Leatham had promised (for the duration of the exercises, at least) to be accountable to Skahill and Moon, who were really the only people who could take the decision as to what the convoy should do. However, neither man could take such a decision because they were the only senior commanders involved who knew nothing of what was about to happen.

It was agreed during the post-attack interviews that, if the convoy had been sailing closer to the shoreline, then less damage might have been done and the number of casualties could have been reduced, although this is really a matter of conjecture. Geddes believed that one of the major problems was that no-one, neither himself, nor the Americans had taken any action at all, until it was too late. No-one acted when the warnings were first given; when the tracer fire was first spotted, or when the E-boats were first sighted on radar. Everyone waited until the attack was actually under way, by which time it was too late. It is quite easy to see Geddes's point here. Many of those involved argued that they were slow or reluctant to react because they believed that everything they were seeing was part of the exercise and not real. However, this is really irrelevant. The whole point of these exercises was to prepare everyone for the reality, so are these men really suggesting that in the real situation of an enemy attack, they would have been this complacent and that they would have just waited to see if anything 'real' materialised? Exercise Tiger was all about training the officers, rather than training the men and in this—at least in part—it failed. Many of the officers waited too long to take vital and necessary action; failed to respond to what was happening around them (whether real or part of the exercise) and showed themselves to be lacking in judgement at the crucial moment.

One of the difficulties with regard to the immediate reactions of the participants might have been that there had been so many different exercises during the weeks and months leading up to Exercise Tiger, that everyone was becoming rather fed up with them and they were finding it hard to take them as seriously as, perhaps, they ought to have done. It would seem that, possibly, in adopting this somewhat casual attitude towards the exercise, the actual purpose involved may have been forgotten. An exercise on this scale was intended as a rehearsal for the real thing and, in the event of an attack having happened on D-Day, it seems fair to say that more direct action would almost certainly have been taken. In the course of an exercise or rehearsal, those involved should behave and react as though everything is happening for real; they should not remain inert, on the basis that they are only taking part in a 'dry run', thereby believing that their reactions do not matter. If that were the case, there would be very little point in practicing operations at all.

Finally, in his interview, Geddes confirmed that the *Azalea* had not picked up any survivors. He stated that his duty, according to his orders, was to protect the remaining ships in the convoy until such time as he could be certain they were no longer in danger from the enemy.

In his interview with Moon, Commander Joseph Skahill confirmed that, while he had no radio contact with either HMS *Azalea* or the Royal Naval bases on the shore, he did have the ability to contact the other LSTs in the convoy. He admitted, however, that he did not contact them until the attack was well underway and felt that he had been remiss in waiting as long as he did. He should, he said, have verified exactly what was happening further back in the convoy. He had been uncertain as to what was taking place, had assumed that the burning LST-507 was not one of his ships and had taken no action. He further admitted that he felt that he should have opened fire on the E-boats when they were first sighted and that he should have ordered the remaining LSTs to scatter earlier in the attack. Skahill made a point of commending the commanding officer of LST-289, Lieutenant Harry Mettler, for getting his ship safely back to port in Dartmouth, despite the serious damage done to her stern. He also praised the commanding officer of LST-515 (on which Skahill himself had been travelling), Lieutenant John Doyle, for returning to the scene of the attack to collect survivors. This praise came in spite of the fact that, at the time, Skahill and Doyle had argued as to whether they ought to return, with some eye-witnesses stating that Skahill threatened Doyle with a court-martial if he did not take the ship into port.

Once compiled, all of these interviews and reports were passed up the line to Rear-Admiral Alan Kirk, US Commander, Western Naval Task Force, whose initial reaction was to blame the British, for failing to provide a sufficiently strong escort to screen the convoy. When later asked why the US Navy had not supplied their own ships for this task, Kirk claimed that had they done so, the Royal Navy would have been angered by such interference and that they would have wanted to take control of the American ships, as well as their own. If the Americans genuinely believed, prior to sailing, that the convoy was under-protected, it seems disgraceful that petty politics—whether perceived or genuine—on the part of both sides, was allowed to get in the way of the convoy's safety. However, both the Americans and the British were equally keen to point out that, despite the frequent warnings of potential E-boat attacks in the Channel that had been given prior to the launch of Exercise Tiger, everyone believed that the risk was minimal and they were only taking part in a practice run.

After having read all of the reports, Kirk requested that a naval bombardment should be aimed at Cherbourg, to eliminate the E-boats as a threat during the forthcoming Normandy landings. He sent this suggestion in a message on 4 May, to his senior officer, the Allied Naval Commander, Expeditionary Force, Rear-Admiral Sir Bertram Ramsay, together with a proposal that the Royal Navy Home Command should reinforce their Plymouth and Portsmouth bases with additional ships to deal with any future E-boat attacks. This later proposal was impossible to fulfil as the Royal Navy simply did not have sufficient vessels to accommodate it.

At that time, perhaps more so than at any other during the war, it was vitally important to maintain Anglo-American relations. However, in the circumstances surrounding the E-boat attack and its aftermath, it was also natural and understandable for each side to hold the other at least partially responsible for events. One of the most difficult senior military relationships at that point was the one between Rear-Admirals Ramsay and Kirk. Ramsay had already antagonised the US Navy and Kirk in particular, by issuing incredibly detailed orders immediately before Exercise Tiger began. The release of these orders was so late in the day that there was insufficient time for the US Naval officers to read or implement them. Almost worse than this, though, was the fact that the US Navy was not accustomed to working with such detailed instructions and resented being told, with quite so much precision, how they should behave in every circumstance, in minute detail. In the US Navy, it was left to individual commanders to make their own decisions, depending on the circumstances and situations that they faced. They took Ramsay's instructions—which were standard for the Royal Navy—to mean that he did not trust them to act under their own authority, without referring up the chain of command, ultimately to their British superiors, such as Ramsay himself.

Kirk's suggestion that the E-boat pens at Cherbourg should be bombarded and put out of action prior to D-Day was not well received by Ramsay, who believed that such an action would be a waste of naval resources. Thus rejected, Kirk decided to go over Ramsay's head to Eisenhower, who then pressed Ramsay for a more meaningful response to the problem. Ramsay held his ground, stating that to mount a raid against heavily defended Cherbourg would risk the lives of too many of his men and their valuable ships, neither of which could be spared in the attempt. The E-boats had, at that time, posed little threat in the Channel and Ramsay saw no reason to waste men and ships on this matter unless, he stated, Eisenhower specifically ordered him to undertake such an action. In this way, Ramsay was passing the responsibility for what he felt would be a foolhardy operation to Eisenhower, meaning that if he was ordered to launch a bombardment and it went wrong, he could always pass the blame onto someone else.

What really angered Ramsay in all of this, however, was not that Eisenhower questioned his opinion, but that Kirk had circumvented the chain of command in order to get his own way. Ramsay saw this as not only unprofessional but took it as a personal slight. Kirk's actions and Ramsay's response could not fail to damage the relations between the British and American navies at a vital time.

Nonetheless, there was no time for accusations of foul-play or personal vendettas. Exercise Fabius was complete and everyone's attention was focused on D-Day.

As part of the preparations for the Normandy landings and specifically those onto Utah beach, the inquisition into Exercise Tiger had to continue, in case anything vital could be learned and applied to the way in which the troops and equipment were landed. All of the Exercise Tiger reports were sent on by Rear-Admiral Kirk to Admiral Harold Stark, the Commander of US Naval Forces in European Waters and they eventually arrived in Washington, on the desk of the Chief of Naval Operations, Admiral Ernest King. One of his first actions was to appoint Rear-Admiral Bernhard Bieri to the staff of the Supreme Commander, which allowed Eisenhower to, in turn, send Bieri as his liaison officer in Ramsay's office. This appointment helped to 'smooth the waves', at least metaphorically, but it also gave the US Navy a friendly presence in Ramsay's department that had been sorely lacking until that point. Bieri's first job was to locate and procure LSTs to replace the two that had been sunk and LST-289 that would take some time to repair. The replacements were required by D-Day, now only a few weeks away and, therefore, building new ships in America was not an option. It was decided that the best course of action was to transfer three vessels from the Mediterranean theatre, where their presence, while important, was not quite so pressing as it was in northern Europe.

Overall, the outcomes of the reports into Exercise Tiger, showed that no one individual was to blame for what had happened, although Skahill and Geddes came in for some criticism. So, for example, the commander of LST-499 had stated in his report that, although the LSTs were ordered to scatter, no rendezvous point was given, which caused confusion. This order was Skahill's responsibility and it was believed that he executed it poorly. Moon was not criticised, but it was felt that there were several factors which conspired against the convoy as a whole. The first and most important of these was the lack of proper communications. This was not due to an error in typing out the radio frequencies as has often been reported, but was simply because neither side had co-ordinated with the other. The end result of this lack of communication was that all parties reacted too slowly to events. The shore bases could not notify the LSTs of the impending attack and neither could Geddes aboard HMS *Azalea*. Equally, Skahill could not communicate with Geddes, so the *Azalea* did not turn back to the scene of the attack until it was too late. Looking back, although one could say that it was the responsibility of Geddes and Skahill to coordinate their communications, it is difficult to see why Moon was not chastised for failing to ensure this simple element. He was in charge of the exercise as a whole and, surely, should have made certain prior to sailing that all of the ships, whether American or British, were able to impart information backwards and forwards.

At the same time, it was agreed between all parties—in common with many survivors—that another major contributing factor in the tragedy was that the LSTs were new to Great Britain, with crews that were barely trained and were carrying army personnel, most of whom had never participated in an amphibious landing and had not been trained in what to do in the event of an attack at sea. These men were not yet ready for combat and neither were their officers, which is why they were taking part in exercises in the first place. This inexperience was, according to the military authorities, a telling factor in some of the mistakes that occurred.

When Admiral Stark saw these accounts, he noted in his report to Admiral King that the Royal Navy had been operating within its normal guidelines. The difference for the British this time, he pointed out, was the involvement of the Americans and their differing systems of working in terms of communications and orders. Both navies had behaved as though they were two separate entities, rather than acting together as one and this would need to be rectified if the landings at Normandy were to be successful.

Although there were no naval dismissals or demotions as a direct result of the E-boat attack, there was—surprisingly—one senior army officer who paid a price. Colonel Eugene Caffey was the Commander of the 1st Engineer Special Brigade and, when his men failed to arrive on Slapton Sands, thus causing confusion and a backlog of equipment, General Omar Bradley was not impressed. Although Bradley was informed at the time of the E-boat attack, he was not told of its severity until after the war, so he blamed Caffey for what happened and ordered General Collins, as Commander of US 7th Corps, to replace Caffey. This was an action which Bradley seems to have later regretted, but his regrets came too late for Caffey, whose military career was blighted by this event, which was no fault of his own.

While recommending to King that 'no further action is contemplated', Stark seems to have failed to take into consideration the feelings of the men who had survived the E-boat attack. A great many of them saw the exercise—quite rightly—as an American affair, with Britain's role being merely to provide the escort vessels which, in the eyes of many survivors, they failed to do. The disappearance of HMS *Scimitar* and the late arrival of HMS *Saladin* would not have prevented the attack from taking place, but having another ship close by would almost certainly have meant that more men could be rescued from the sea. In looking closer to home, at the American role in the tragedy, the survivors, whether naval or army personnel—and with few exceptions—remained incredulous that most of the army men were not properly trained in certain basic elements of sea-faring knowledge. Had they been properly trained this might have resulted in fewer lives being lost.

While these factors have led to anger and bitterness among the veterans, perhaps the aspect that outrages them more than any other, is the supposed secrecy and perceived deception which many of them believe was practised by the US military and government. There are several survivors who tell stories of the families of the victims of the E-boat attack, claiming that they were not told of the circumstances of their loved-ones' deaths for years. This accusation has been embellished over the years to the point where some maintain that the families were actually not even told at all that their loved ones had even died—let alone being told how, when or where.

The former suggestion is feasible—at least to a certain extent. In the same way as the survivors were forced to keep quiet about the attack for security reasons, it was equally important that secrecy be maintained at home in America. At the time, families were told that their husband/son/father/brother had been 'killed in action in the performance of his duty and the service of his country' and that his remains had been 'interred in Allied territory outside continental limits of the United States pending cessation of hostilities'. The families were promised further information when it became available, but were told not to reveal the name of the deceased's ship 'to prevent possible aid to our enemies'.

The suggestion that the truth was never revealed to the families, or that it took years, or decades for them to discover what had happened in some sort of glorified government cover-up, is given the lie by the newspaper reports that began to appear not long after D-Day, giving details of the E-boat attack. One such example explains that Seaman First-Class Edwin James Dobson, who had been on board LST-531, had been reported missing following action on 28 April, stating that he was 'a member of the crew serving on board a vessel that, while en route to an exercise area in the English Channel, was sunk by enemy E-boats'. This information, the report goes on, had been given to his mother by the Navy Department. Equally, John Brown and Raymond Gosselin were writing to Lieutenant John Hill's family back in America within months of the E-boat attack. Both men were giving details of the event and John Brown also sent photographs of the grave markers at Brookwood Cemetery. The fact that none of these letters sent home by Brown or Gosselin, giving details of Exercise Tiger were censored makes a mockery of any suggestion of a blanket official cover-up. If the authorities had been so keen to keep the truth hidden, there is no way that they would have permitted these documents and, especially, their enclosed photographs to reach their destination. The truth of the matter is that, while some survivors shared their experiences with their own families and others, some men chose to remain silent and assumed that everyone else had—including the authorities who had ordered their silence in the first place.

E-BOAT VICTIM — Seaman First Class Edwin James Dobson, who was earlier reported missing in action since April 28, was a member of the crew serving on board a vessel that, while en route to an exercise area in the English Channel, was sunk by enemy E-Boats, the Navy Department revealed in a recent letter to his mother, Mrs. Edna Berry Dobson of 1125 Lisbon Street.

There has been no change in the status of Seaman Dobson, Navy Department officials told Mrs. Dobson, since the original message notifying her that he was missing.

He enjoyed a long visit with his father, Pharmacist's Mate Bailey C. Dobson, in England only four days before he was lost, Mrs. Dobson said.

Newspaper report giving details of the death of Edwin James Dobson. Clipping courtesy of Beverly Hughes.

There are many official notifications and letters offering varying degrees of detail about what happened to Convoy T-4 on 28 April, making it quite hard to believe the stories that no-one was told anything at all about what happened. What one might be able to argue, is that the families were not given very much information or detail about precisely what happened to their own specific relations, or the exact circumstances of their deaths. However, it must also be said that there is every possibility that the authorities themselves were as much in the dark as everyone else in some cases. One of the biggest problems appears to have been that some of the newspaper reports only really aided to confuse, giving false or inaccurate details, such as one, which stated that Lieutenant John Hill had died in the Atlantic. Then, the employees' magazine for the company at which Lieutenant Hill had worked issued an article in praise former employees who had fallen in the line of duty. They give a description of Hill as having perished 'when an ammunition boat exploded in the Mediterranean area'. Aspects such as this did little to help families, many of whom were still trying to come to terms with their losses, as well as finding out what had happened to their loved-ones.

Some survivors have stated that there are victims of Exercise Tiger who have not been listed as such, but who have been incorporated into the casualty numbers for the Normandy landings. As with the 'massaging' of the figures, it is difficult to see why the authorities would want to do this. For both events, the number of dead was already high enough. What would be the value or purpose in pretending that either figure was higher or lower than the reality?

In such situations, when men have died for no valuable reason, those who are left behind, whether they are the bereaved relatives, or the survivors of the event, often search for someone to blame and, in this case, that became the US government and military authorities, who were deemed by some to have kept the families deliberately in the dark. By the time much of the finer detail regarding Exercise Tiger did come to light, quite a few of the loved ones at home had died themselves, especially in the case of the parents of the soldiers and sailors who had perished. This, in turn led to feelings of resentment among many of the survivors, that some family members might have gone to their graves without really knowing the truth.

Such thoughts made some veterans want to seek justice for their fallen comrades and it also led to and fuelled some of the theories of a great military cover-up surrounding the whole event, exaggerated into suggestions that reports had been falsified, that officers had lied to cover their supposed 'guilt' (although what they were meant to be guilty of is unclear) and that everyone from Eisenhower down, knew about the betrayal of the dead men and were instrumental in perpetuating it.

One of the men who wanted to know more about the event was Ralph Greene, who had been a doctor, serving at the 228th Station Hospital at Sherborne in Dorset. He had always been haunted by the men who had passed through his hands and the hospital that night, as well as the orders he had received as to how the survivors were to be treated and that nothing

Employees' Magazine ✦✦✦ July 1944   7

IN SERVICE 3,334   DEAD 32   MISSING 2

★★★ OUR MILITARY RECORD ★★★

Three more Boston and Maine employees were reported killed in war service the past month — one in an explosion at sea, the other two during training maneuvers in this country — bringing to 32 the total of our Honored Dead.

New Gold Stars

✮   ✮   ✮

Lt. (jg) John H. Hill, USN.
Arlington, Mass.
Pvt. Henry F. O'Connell, USA.
Somerville, Mass.
Cadet Hugh E. Crawford, USAAF.
West Roxbury, Mass.

Lt. Hill, formerly a machinist in the Charlestown enginehouse, died when an ammunition boat exploded in the Mediterranean area; Pvt. O'Connell, former laborer at the same enginehouse, was wounded fatally during maneuvers at Camp Breckinbridge, Ky.; and Aviation Cadet Crawford, former clerk in the Purchasing Department at Boston, was killed when his plane crashed near Shaw Field, S. C.

transferred in 1930 to the Charlestown enginehouse. He entered the Navy in July, 1942, as a first-class machinist and subsequently was promoted to Lieutenant, junior grade. He was married and had one child.

Cadet Crawford, 19, had nearly completed his basic training at Shaw Field when he was killed. He entered railroad employ May 1, 1942, and nine months later enlisted in the Army Air Forces. After five months in the College Training Detachment at Syracuse University, he was qualified for pilot training. He received initial training at Maxwell Field, Ala., and Palmer Field, S. C., before going to Shaw Field for basic training. He leaves a younger brother, Ralph, in the Navy, and his next of kin is an uncle, E. J. Scott.

Saville   O'Connell

Pvt. O'Connell, also 19, entered our employ May 4, 1943, at the new terminal, and only three weeks later was called to military service. He was killed by accidental shooting while training, according to the War Department report to his parents, Mr. and Mrs. Henry F. O'Connell.

Pictured with O'Connell is Ensign Kenneth W. Saville, former B. and M. employee, whose death was reported in our June issue. He was a brakeman on the Portland Division and the son of Fireman Thomas Saville of that Division. He was killed in combat while piloting a naval bomber in the Pacific.

Hill   Crawford

Lt. Hill, 39, was killed April 28. He entered railroad service at Billerica in March, 1921; transferred to Somerville as machinist helper in 1923, became a machinist in 1926, and was

Article from the Employees' Magazine of the company where Lt John Hill worked, giving details of the employees who had been killed during that month. *Clipping courtesy of Beverly Hughes* should be said about their presence. Only a long time after the war did he discover what had really happened that night and, like Eugene Eckstam, Ralph Greene decided to find out the truth. When, in 1974, the Freedom of Information Act allowed access to the reports about the exercise, Greene travelled to Washington to study the documents in the archives. Through his discoveries and quest to know more, Greene was instrumental in reuniting many of the survivors and in helping to bring Exercise Tiger into the public eye. However, in doing so, he also helped to fuel the conspiracy theories and rumours, maintaining that the thirty years of silence, which is applicable to all such military activities, actually amounted to a cover-up. Greene also implied that this supposed cover-up suggested that the E-boat attack might actually have cost more lives than the authorities had admitted and these findings formed the basis of many of the subsequent stories which have raged on for the ensuing forty years, ever since Greene opened the first of those archival boxes and the can of worms inside.

The survivors' need to find someone to blame was always going to be fruitless and they were, therefore, always going to keep searching in their attempt to find a scapegoat but, with regard to the actual E-boat attack, while some blame was apportioned, no-one was actually punished because although errors were definitely made, no-one was really prepared for an E-boat attack at that time, so close to mainland Britain, carried out with such speed and precision. It could be said that, although there were errors of judgement, planning and execution, the Germans, on that occasion, got lucky. Many of the oversights and mistakes are easy to see and criticise with the benefit of hindsight and the knowledge of what was to happen that night, but many of these problems were rectified in time for D-Day, ensuring that the casualty figures on Utah Beach were less than half of those in Exercise Tiger. Nonetheless, this was an expensive lesson and one that, from the perspective of those affected, was neither right nor fair; but then it is also worth bearing in mind that war has never been acknowledged as being just or reasonable.

CHAPTER NINE

'It's a Lovely Day Tomorrow'

The long-term effects of Exercise Tiger on the survivors

Among the survivors of Exercise Tiger, there was not just a natural desire to blame, mingled with the accompanying anger and bitterness; there was also confusion as to how and why the tragedy had been allowed to happen in the first place and what had caused so many men to die in a seemingly pointless cause. There was grief over fallen comrades, the feelings of guilt that often surround the survivors of such events and the fear and recurring nightmares as men relived the horrific events of that night, over and over again.

Some of the veterans would eventually channel these feelings into their work and, upon returning home after the war, they either took up, or continued with their careers, whether in the military, or in civilian occupations. A great many of them were very young and returned to education, in the hope of bettering themselves in the future, perhaps with the ambition of achieving something tangible in memory of their lost friends. Many of the veterans married, quite often to their sweethearts or fiancées from before the war and they went on to have families of their own, although in a great many cases, these families remained oblivious to the events that had occurred during the war. Some of the American survivors developed an obsession with finding out the truth and searching for other veterans, so that the real story of Exercise Tiger could be told. Most of the men said nothing about that tragedy of that night for many years to come and some took their 'secret' story to their graves. For others, the feeling of release to finally speak out only came several decades later, when the exercise came more into the public eye and they realised that it was now permitted for them to reveal their version of events. Until that point, the years passed in silence and, for all except those who had taken part, Exercise Tiger was a largely forgotten episode.

For some of the survivors, the personal memories of what they had witnessed that night would haunt them for the rest of their lives. After the war, Eugene

Eckstam continued to serve in the US Navy until 1946 and remained in the Reserves until 1954, by which time he had qualified as a civilian surgeon. Completing his surgical residency in 1950, Dr Eckstam embarked on a long and highly respected career. Throughout this time and his retirement, which he devoted to discovering the truth about the exercise, and right up to his death in 2010, Eckstam carried the burden of his memory of the impossible position in which he had been placed on LST-507. His vivid recollection of having to close one of the tank deck hatches, locking in the men who were inside the burning void, while being able to hear their screams for help, would become the stuff of nightmares. The knowledge that he was adhering to Navy regulations and that to leave the hatch open could endanger the ship and the lives of many other men on board, offered Eckstam some solace, but he would always be plagued by the sounds of those men screaming to be saved, while they burned and the knowledge that there was nothing he could do to help them.

Angelo Crapanzano returned home after the war to marry his sweetheart, Ida, whose letters to him had been lost when LST-507 was sunk. The couple went on to have two daughters and Crapanzano became an apprentice in the die-making department of a folding box business. Over the years, he was promoted within the company, until he became the foreman of his department. Despite his professional progress, Crapanzano recalls that after the war, he was 'never the same man again', adding that he was unable to feel really happy about anything. He found it impossible to speak to anyone about his experiences and this led to a breakdown in 1961, which saw him hospitalised. Crapanzano believed, rightly or wrongly, that it was not really until the Vietnam War that doctors in America began to fully understand the long-term effects of combat fatigue and Post Traumatic Stress Disorder although, at the time, he firmly felt that his problem stemmed from what had happened to him during Exercise Tiger and his inability to talk about it afterwards. Having been awarded the Bronze Star for rescuing his shipmate John McGarigal and then keeping him afloat for several hours until help arrived, Crapanzano felt ill-used by the authorities who, in his view, had wanted to brush the whole affair under the carpet. In recalling his fallen comrades, the manner of their deaths and their subsequent treatment, while giving his oral account of his experiences, Crapanzano breaks down on several occasions: the emotions, even several decades later, still very raw.

Crapanzano's breakdown took years to materialise, but for him and many others, there would also be more immediate effects and problems occurring as a direct result of their involvement and experiences in Exercise Tiger. Crapanzano himself, like most of the other men, was not allowed any shore leave and was, almost immediately, assigned to another LST in preparation for crossing the Channel on D-Day. As a Motor Machinist's Mate (First Class), when he went on board his new ship, LST-294, Crapanzano was naturally given his usually duty in the main engine room—exactly the same as it had been on LST-507. This meant taking up the same position as he had been in when the torpedo had struck his former ship. Crapanzano reported to the engineering officer, who knew about Exercise Tiger and some of what had happened and he asked Crapanzano if he was ready and willing to undertake this duty. Crapanzano believed that he could cope with the situation, so agreed to accompany the officer to the engine room. However, when the two men arrived there, Crapanzano began to panic and, realising what was wrong, the engineering officer immediately took him up on deck, before going to speak to the ship's executive officer. Upon his return, the engineering officer explained to Crapanzano that it had been arranged for him to be re-assigned and that he would be working with the engineering officer, taking care of the records in the engine room office. His station during General Quarters had also been changed from the engine room, to manning a gun on deck. With the help of this understanding officer, Crapanzano was able to avoid facing the terrible reality—even if only for a brief time—that he had been the only man from the engine room of LST-507, to make it out alive.

A similar fate awaited Patsy Giacchi when he was re-assigned to the 94th Quartermaster Railhead Company and sent to a new LST for transportation to Normandy. Giacchi had been expecting at least a brief spell of leave, but instead was transferred to Brixham, from where he and his comrades had originally embarked on Exercise Tiger on board LST-507. As the truck carrying the troops arrived at the port, Giacchi was filled with a sense of panic as he was hit by the smell of oil and gasoline that seemed to pervade the area, reminding him of the night of the E-boat attack. On D-Day itself, once the LST carrying Giacchi and his company was underway, he found that he could not bear to be below decks, so he stood topside in the fresh air and, what he considered to be relative safety. At one stage, an officer approached and asked Giacchi why he was not below with the other men, to which Giacchi simply replied: 'I'm one of the survivors'. No other comment or explanation was necessary for the officer to understand the situation and offer to help Giacchi.

The effects on the survivors were not only emotional or psychological. Some men also suffered from physical difficulties for many months or years after the event. There were the obvious cases of men who had lost limbs, those who were burns victims, had received gun shot and shrapnel wounds, men who had suffered from hypothermia and exposure and the effects of swallowing too much oil-laden water, to name but a few of the long-lasting medical problems. Some men were treated in England, patched up and sent back to their ships or army units, others were repatriated back to America for more intensive, long-term care. For some of the wounded, their injuries signalled the end of their war, but their on-going treatment would last many more months and, sometimes, years afterwards. Among the most severe and saddest of such cases, is the story of twenty-one year old Private (First Class) Henry Victor Martin Jr., who had been on board LST-507 serving, like Patsy Giacchi, with the 557th Quartermaster Railhead Company. After the explosion and the order to abandon ship, Martin had jumped overboard and was later pulled from the water with what appeared to be minor injuries. He was taken to hospital where the doctors told him that he was only suffering from flesh wounds and that no x-rays were necessary. He complained, at the time, of being in extreme pain, but was told that this was psychological. Despite his injuries and his pain, Martin was treated and sent back out to participate in the D-Day landings. After the war, he returned to America, where he married and raised his own family, although he continued to live in terrible pain. It was not until 1959 that an x-ray revealed that there were, in fact, two bullets lodged either side of his spine, which accounted for the 'psychological' pain that he had suffering from, for some fifteen years. In May of the following year, it was arranged for him to have surgery to remove these bullets, at the Veterans Hospital in Houston, thus freeing him from the pain that had made most of his adult life a misery. Martin was due to be transferred to the hospital on the 10th of May, but he passed away the day before, aged just thirty-seven years old. Despite the pain he suffered, his daughter recalls that 'he never complained' and that she learned the reality of his situation, not from her father, but from her grandfather.

There was another victim of the effects of Exercise Tiger—although, perhaps, some veterans might disagree with the portrayal of him as a victim and hold him at least partially responsible for what happened to them and their comrades. That man was Rear-Admiral Don P. Moon. After the exercises were completed, the reports filed and Moon exonerated of blame in the tragedy, in common with the other commanders, he turned his attention to the D-Day landings, during which he commanded 'Force U' from USS *Bayfield*. There were no E-boat attacks during the landings, but some of the LSTs were damaged or sunk by mines, as they approached the French coast and on one occasion, a vessel was 'blown completely in half, sinking rapidly'. In this instance, unlike during Exercise Tiger, the USS *Bayfield* was on hand and close enough to rescue the survivors of the stricken ship.

USS *Bayfield* remained off Utah Beach for three weeks after the first landings, helping with some of the wounded and the continuing arrival of further men and supplies as the infantry advanced into northern France. Then, in early July, the ship set sail for Naples, where planning was already underway for Operation Dragoon—the invasion into southern Europe, which was due to begin on 15 August. On the night of 5 August, while in his cabin, Rear-Admiral Moon wrapped a towel around his .45 calibre pistol and shot himself, thus becoming the first flag officer of the United States Navy to take his own life while in combat.

Moon's suicide was officially blamed on 'combat fatigue', but the officers around him, who had actually served with him throughout, believed that there was more to it than that. Moon was a very intense, hard-working officer, who slept little and many of his fellow officers, who saw him both during and after Exercise Tiger, noted the strain under which he was working. The enquiries into the E-boat attack had found that he bore no blame for what had happened, but that does not mean that he did not feel any responsibility within himself—as many senior officers would in such circumstances, regardless of their actual culpability. Despite the findings of the immediate enquiries, there were rumours that there might have to be a further board of enquiry which would be held later in America, at which Rear-Admiral Moon would have to account for his role in the disaster. It seems unlikely that, taken in isolation, the E-boat attack and its tragic aftermath would have had any major consequences, in terms of Moon's career or reputation. However, a more important aspect to consider is the incident of 27 April, in which an unquantified number of American soldiers were killed by 'friendly fire'. This episode would almost certainly have been scrutinised by the board of enquiry and the deaths involved occurred, arguably, as a result of the decision made by Moon, to postpone that day's H-Hour from 07.30 to 08.30 and the failure of that command to reach all necessary units. Moon cannot be held entirely liable for the failures in communication but, as a result, some men landed on the beach ahead of time and walked straight into a live bombardment. If one is looking for a contributory factor in Moon's suicide, this would seem the more likely as, while he may not have been responsible for the deaths caused by the E-boat attack, the casualties as a result of the 'friendly fire' incident were ones for which he would have had to account and for which—rightly or wrongly—he might well have felt an element of guilt. Whatever Moon's reasons for committing suicide and whether or not they were related to Exercise Tiger in any way, will now never be known. The indisputable fact is that he left behind a wife, Sybil, and four children—Meredith, Don, David and Peter—who, like many others at home, could only grieve for the loss of a beloved husband and father.

Those affected by Exercise Tiger and its aftermath were not limited to the American soldiers and sailors and their families at home. The British contingent was sometimes equally haunted by their own experiences, although there were obviously fewer military participants to feel the effects. In the immediate aftermath, for example, Lieutenant-Commander Geddes from HMS *Azalea* had said nothing to his family about what had happened. However, in later years, it became clear that he was, indeed, troubled by the disaster, describing it as 'horrendous' and 'a tragedy'. John Cullen, the Second Coxswain from HMRML 532, who had pulled so many bodies from the sea during the morning of 28 April, described himself as feeling 'sick, not physically, but really depressed as the memory of what happened kept crossing my mind'.

The effects were not just felt among the military. Slapton Sands had been evacuated to enable the exercises to take place and those who had abandoned their homes would also feel the consequences of these events.

Once D-Day had come and gone, the villages around Slapton Sands that had been evacuated and taken over by the US Army, were once again deserted. By this stage, however, the evacuated population had already begun to suffer quite severe hardships. Their homes and, in many cases, their livelihoods, had been taken from them, with very little notice, for an unspecified and unpredictable amount of time. For some, it had been difficult to find alternative employment and there were quite a number of families who were sharing accommodation with others, while their furniture remained in storage. Financially, as well as socially, times were extremely hard for these families and many were struggling to make ends meet and, while for the younger generation, the evacuation was still being seen as an adventure, for most of the adults concerned, it was becoming a very worrying time.

Over six months had passed since they had left their homes, farms and businesses and, with the invasion now underway, they were still uncertain as to exactly when they would be allowed to return to their villages and—perhaps even more worryingly—what they might find when they got there.

Although the Normandy Landings had begun on 6 June, it was not until nearly a month later, on 4 July, that an announcement was made to the effect that the requisitioned area of the South Hams could be handed back by the American Military, to the British civilian authorities. Despite the relief of this good news, the villagers were to face further disappointment when they discovered that even then there were to be delays, the first of which was that the US Army had to ensure that all of their arms and equipment had been safely removed from the vicinity. Then, the electricity supply had to be reconnected and food distribution organised. Additionally, there was the matter of the damage done to the roads, which had to be repaired before any civilians could be allowed back into the area.

While all of this was going on, the evacuees, waiting with growing impatience in nearby towns and villages, were brutally aware that as time passed, the chances of growing valuable and necessary crops in the fields and kitchen gardens during that year were lessening and that their properties and farms were becoming more and more derelict with every passing week. The local Member of Parliament, Colonel Ralph Rayner, had been petitioning, since the initial evacuation, for suitable compensation for the evacuees and now his voice was joined by newspapers and local councillors, one of whom commented that 'the whole country has benefitted by the sacrifices of these people and, therefore, it was only fair that the whole country should put their hands in their pockets and help in the rehabilitation'.

Although everyone felt certain that, deep down, the evacuated civilians would feel a very justified sense of pride that their personal sacrifices had resulted in a direct and positive effect on the successful invasion, no amount of pride was going to pay for the repairs to each individuals' buildings, fences, walls, gates and hedges.

Having failed to gain much sympathy from the British Government, who always fell back on the limited terms of the Defence Regulations and Compensation Act of 1939, Rayner turned instead to the Americans, asking if they would provide compensation to those civilians who had been turned out of their properties. However, not long after opening his negotiations, Rayner was ordered by the British Government to cease his discussions with the Americans, as it was not considered politically expedient at the time. Despite Rayner's withdrawal, the Americans did set aside £6,000 as a contingency fund to meet the requirements of the most urgent and needy civilian cases.

Slowly but surely, preparations and general repairs were made. Beginning on 19 August, at East Allington, the villagers started to return to their homes. Some found surprisingly little change, other than, perhaps, a very thick layer of dust, extremely overgrown gardens and fields and the occasional broken window. For others, the damage was much worse and, in some cases, was heart-breaking. Firstly there was the destruction caused by the bombardments that had been carried out during the exercises. Some of this was to private dwellings, but also to the churches, possibly because they had given the gunners a good target to aim at. Worse than any of this, though, was the more 'man-made' vandalism, in which properties—usually individual homes—had been defaced, with door and window frames removed and used for firewood; fittings wrecked and walls daubed with obscene language and images. Some indoor rooms had quite clearly been used as latrines, where the properties only had outdoor facilities, so effectively the troops had created their own, more warm and comfortable version, inside the houses. Having been told that the American soldiers would be housed in camps and would not be permitted inside private dwellings, the returning owners and occupants were doubly angry—not only about what they had found, but also about the broken promises which they had been given. A few complained about what they had discovered, but were usually told to keep their views to themselves, for fear of upsetting the relationship between the Allies.

These findings did little to endear the Americans to a small population, already somewhat fed-up with what they perceived to be an 'occupation' by a foreign force. This relationship had already been strained by an incident in May, just before the Normandy Landings began, when two boys were killed having discovered an unexploded grenade, while playing just outside the evacuation area. For some of the locals, already growing resentful of their displacement, the deaths of these two innocents added to their anger and misery.

It must be said, however, that the level of damage which some experienced, with its accompanying anger and distress, was not a universal experience, and that the majority of the 3,000 evacuees returned home to find that very little harm had been done to their houses, other than what might normally be expected from leaving a property empty and unattended for eight months or more.

In late 1944, Herbert Luscombe, the blacksmith from Stokenham, returned to his smithy from nearby Beeson, where he had been sharing the workload of that village's blacksmith. Upon his return to Stokenham, Luscombe took up residence in his cottage next to his shop and was soon back at work.

The Hannaford family, who owned the butcher's shop in Torcross, found that a great deal had changed upon their return from Chivelstone, where they had spent the previous months. Firstly, the family car, which they had been forced to leave behind in the evacuation, was missing and was later found in Slapton Ley. The yard to the rear of the family shop had been used as a tank park and one of the large butcher's blocks was discovered burned beyond redemption. Outbuildings had been demolished and there was a great deal of glass lying around the property from all the broken windows. Having already experienced the upheaval of trying to set up a new, temporary business in Prawle, with no electricity in their premises, the family must have looked forward to returning to their normal lives. These discoveries must have made that return very disappointing.

At the time of the evacuation, Freda Luscombe had not gone with the rest of her family to Littlehempston, but had moved into the farm owned by the family of her fiancé, Tony Widger, and the couple had then married in May 1944. Although Freda's family residence, Sloutt's Farm, was not too badly damaged, Poole Farm, which was to become Freda and Tony's home after the evacuation, was in need of some repair to make it habitable. The move back to Sloutt's Farm took place in November 1944, but it was February of the following year before Tony and Freda could move into their new home at Poole Farm. In common with most of the farmers, they found that one of the biggest problems they faced on their return was the number of rabbits in the area, whose presence made it almost impossible to grow anything until their numbers could be brought back under control.

Some of the rabbits were dealt with by the children of the Bowles family, who caught them around the village and in the farms and fields, before selling them to other villagers. This family had moved from Slapton to Milton Farm in Dartmouth, and they were able to move back in the autumn of 1944, to what young Eddie Bowles described as a 'ghost town'.

For some of the inhabitants, the condition of their properties upon their eventual return was not so much of a surprise. Builder, Godfrey Wills, was one such person, as in his role in the Observer Corps, he had been allowed a permit to pass through his own village of Strete to Start Point, where his unit was based. This was only given to him once the exercises were completed and the Americans had departed but, Wills was still able to see, prior to his return in the autumn of 1944, that his own property had sustained little damage, except for a few broken windows. Nonetheless, it must have been very frustrating for him to be able to cycle past his house, but not go inside, or stay there. As a builder, when he did return, Godfrey Wills found himself in great demand over the coming weeks and months, as the inhabitants of the nearby villages tried to rebuild their homes, as well as their lives. Settling back into their villages was something which they had looked forward to for many long months and now that it was finally happening, the people of Slapton and the surrounding villages began to look forward to a brighter and more peaceful tomorrow.

CHAPTER TEN

'Sentimental Journey'

An examination of various conspiracy theories

Whilst undoubtedly a military exercise, with procedures and consequences to match, the E-boat attack of Exercise Tiger and its aftermath also turned it into a very personal, human experience for each of the people involved, which would remain with the survivors for the rest of their lives. It is really this aspect of the event that continues to interest and influence modern enthusiasts and the families of those who participated and, even those historians who take an interest are often swayed in their perspectives by the personal stories of the men who came back. The fact that there are now very few men left to recall the event, makes these narratives all the more important and poignant.

In recounting the individual experiences of their participation in Exercise Tiger, the survivors quite often seem to tell different stories—sometimes of exactly the same incident—which can be confusing for anyone coming upon this event for the first time. So, for example, both Eugene Eckstam and Ed Panter served on LST-507 and were both medical men, as part of 'Foxy 29'. They both left the ship after the order was given, at approximately 02.30, but while Eckstam recalls climbing 'down a cargo net' on his own, Panter gives an account in which both men jumped 'off the stern' of the ship together. Their accounts both give some additional detail: Eckstam remembers the feeling of slowly sinking into the cold water and allowing his inflatable life belt to rise up under his armpits. Panter, on the other hand, tells of a brief conversation, after they had landed in the water, between himself and Eckstam regarding the fact that the latter had, for some reason, brought his gas mask with him and was clinging to it. Eckstam makes no mention of this discussion or the presence of the gas mask. It seems obvious that both men cannot possibly be right and some might argue that, therefore, one of them must either be making up, or embellishing, his version of events. However, that is not necessarily the case. Admittedly, Eckstam cannot have 'jumped off' the ship and climbed 'down the cargo net' at the same time but, by his own admission, he remembers little about what happened and almost nothing after he entered the water, having no recollections of anything until his rescue. Therefore, it is not unreasonable to suppose that the elements which he does remember might be a little hazy. Equally, Panter seems unable to remember his rescue, or very much of what happened after he entered the water, so it is difficult to rely entirely on the accuracy of his account either. That is not to say that these events did not happen, it might simply mean that their sequence or the people involved were different. It is possible, for example, that the two men were together, but that Eckstam had forgotten about Panter's presence or the conversation which they had in the water. It could be that they started to climb down the cargo net and then Panter decided to jump and assumed that Eckstam had followed him. It may be that Panter spoke to someone in the water about a gas mask, but that this man was not Eckstam. From this distance in time, we cannot hope to know, but this slight discrepancy does not make either of these accounts any less interesting.

Any police officer or investigator will always say that each witness to a crime or road traffic accident will offer a slightly—or even drastically—different description of events and participants and this is also the case with anyone who has taken part in an event such as Exercise Tiger. Memories become muddled, especially when they are formed at a time of extreme stress or trauma and then, given many years—or sometimes decades—to develop. At the same time, the accounts of other people can influence a person's own memories of the events which they witnessed, thereby tainting their own reminiscences.

In his account of the event, John Maltese states that the night of 28 April 1944 would 'always stand out' in his mind, before going on to recall that his ship (which he does not identify) left 'Dover' to go to Slapton Sands. However, none of the LSTs which took part in Exercise Tiger departed from Dover (in Kent, in the South East of England); they either embarked from Plymouth or Brixham (both located in Devon, in the South West of England, over 250 miles from Dover). We have to assume, therefore, that Maltese has muddled up his ports with the passage of time and that, with Dover being one of the most famous and iconic symbols of England during the Second World War, with its white cliffs, he has mistakenly named the Kent port. In his account, Maltese later goes on to recall that 'three LSTs went down', meaning that three vessels were sunk during the attack. This erroneous comment could possibly be based on early reports from the time, which mistakenly said that there were three sunken ships, due to the amount of wreckage that was visible in the water. Alternatively, it could be that Maltese believed that LST-289 had been sunk, rather than damaged. In his oral report, Maltese also says that the following day, the water was still burning, the sea was red with blood and bodies were pushed up onto the shore by landing craft. While there is no evidence as to whether this did or did not happen and it cannot be proved either way, no other eyewitness has reported seeing any of these things and during the next day, the exercise was still being carried out, so it is fair to assume that Maltese would have been with his unit at that time, not out at sea, leaving us to wonder whether these 'sights' are really hearsay, embellished over the years, rather than fact.

Finally, Maltese reports that some of the families of the men who lost their lives were not even told about their deaths for many years and then he informs his interviewer that 'Admiral Moon' had committed suicide the very next day, implying in his comments that Moon either bore, or felt, some sense of responsibility or guilt for what had occurred. The former suggestion really does not make sense. It seems implausible that families would be kept in the dark about the actual death of a participant in Exercise Tiger, even if—as some have suggested—the authorities perpetuated the 'silence' regarding the circumstances of these deaths. As to Moon's suicide, that occurred on 5 August, more than three months after the event and, as has already been discussed in the previous chapter, may or may not have been connected with Exercise Tiger. The account of John Maltese was given orally in September 2008, sixty-four years after the E-boat attack, so it is easy to see how a person's recollections may be clouded with the passage of time.

In other cases, there are just minor details and elements of accounts which either do not make sense or do not 'add up', when put into the overall context of the event. One example of this would be Angelo Crapanzano's account of spending four-and-a-half hours in the water before being rescued. Looking more closely at this, if Crapanzano had jumped overboard after the 'abandon ship' order was given, as he states in his version of events, at 02.30 or just after, he would have been rescued after four-and-a-half hours at around 07.00, or probably a little later. Yet, his account of his rescue tells of it being 'still dark' and his seeing a light in the distance, which turned out to be the approaching LST-515. However, at 07.00, it would have been daylight, or at least dawn, confirmed by the fact that John Cullen (Second Coxswain on board HMRML 532) recalled that his vessel was ordered back out to the attack site to search for survivors and pick up bodies from the water at first light—which time he gives as 05.00. There is every chance, therefore, that Crapanzano, perhaps, did not spent quite as long in the water as he was recalling in his interview, given several decades later. It is quite easy to see, however, that in the ice-cold English Channel, two or three hours might easily feel like significantly longer. It must be said here, though, that Crapanzano's account is given some credence by the fact that it is repeated in the recollections of Patsy Giacchi, who reports seeing a light 'in the distance' after spending over four hours in the water. To some, this would make it seem much more likely that Crapanzano is right in his estimate of the time, since both men tell almost identical stories with regard to the timing of their rescues. So perhaps it is Cullen who has got his timings wrong? Or perhaps not. At the beginning of Giacchi's interview, we learn that he had, before coming forward to tell his story, first read Crapanzano's account and, it is not impossible to suppose that some element of the naval man's report, which might have been hazy in Giacchi's mind, could have rubbed off. In any case, this aspect, while not vitally important to the overall story, cannot be ignored when examining their testimonies.

Another survivor, Dale Rodman, claims that he was rescued by HMS *Azalea*, along with dozens of other men. This is despite the fact that the captain of the *Azalea*, Lieutenant-Commander Geddes stated in his official report that he had not stopped to collect any survivors from the water after the E-boat attack, but had remained with the convoy. Geddes was an experienced captain, used to escorting convoys and there would be no reason to suppose that he would lie about his actions. It is quite possible that Rodman was rescued by another British vessel, as others did arrive on the scene within a few hours of the E-boat attack.

Even the accounts of the German S-boote commanders can be seen to vary, especially with regard to the number of torpedoes fired by each vessel, the targets hit and the boats responsible for hitting them and, more especially, the timings of almost everything. When it comes to the matter of timings, one would expect a degree of similarity in the accounts of each commander. So, if we just examine the timing of the S-boote ceasing their attack and subsequent arrivals at Cherbourg following the attack, for example, Korvettenkapitän Klug, who was the commanding officer of the 5th S-Flottille, with six boats under his command, entered into his log that he called off the attack at 03.17. The reason which Klug gives for having taken this action at this very precise time was that one of the vessels under his command was damaged and that he did not wish to endanger the rest of the flotilla. However, the captain of S-*140*, which was part of the 5th S-Flottille and, therefore, under Klug's command, stated in his log that he had left the area at 02.40. Equally, Kapitänleutnant Jürgenmeyer of S-*136*—also under Klug's command—logged that he called off his attack at 01.56, returning to Cherbourg at 03.09. These timings, as well as those for the commencement of the attack and the firing of the torpedoes are at odds with each other and it is difficult to see why this would be the case. Some of these discrepancies, specifically those regarding which S-boot fired torpedoes at which time could easily be mistakes, caused by the fact that the S-boote were operating in different sectors of the attack area, so they may well have observed things from different perspectives. There can certainly be no reason to think that any of the German officers would feel the need to lie or elaborate about their involvement in the attack, or that they would be part of any supposed American secrecy plot or cover-up. The logs were written at the time of the event, so there can be no diminishing of memories with the passing of time. Looking at the matter logically, it is, however, possible that some of the S-boote were acting independently of the command vessel and they may not have been in direct contact with Klug. Such vessels may well have broken off from the main force and returned to port early, once they had fired all of their torpedoes, in order to protect their boats and crews.

Phil Nevill, the fighter-bomber pilot with the Royal Air Force Volunteer Reserve has also provided a few anomalies over which enthusiasts may speculate. Among these was his account of having fired two rockets at an E-boat and then of following it until it 'exploded', implying that one of the E-boats was completely destroyed by his action. However, this does not tic in with any other report, whether German, American or British, all of which state that all nine E-boats made it back to Cherbourg.

The point in all of this analysing of the minutiae surrounding the event is not to be pedantic and neither is it to call into question the veracity or integrity of the testimonies of any of the participants or witnesses, regardless of their nationality. After all, in the grand scheme of things, these minor details and discrepancies matter not a jot, except, that is, when they are taken out of context or in isolation and treated as the only correct and true version of events. The only real problem with these first-hand and eye-witness accounts lies not in their content, but in their treatment by others.

There are some 'historians', enthusiasts and writers (and there is a marked difference between the three types), who read these accounts, believe every single syllable of them unquestioningly, without bothering to research them any further, and assume that any discrepancies automatically indicate a conspiracy of some kind. Equally, they might read just one or two eye-witness accounts in isolation and then assume that any official report which contradicts that account must be part of an orchestrated cover-up, simply because an eye-witness version of events has to be the more accurate, for the simple reason that it was written by someone who was 'there'. The fact that an official report might have been written by someone who was also there and written within days of the event, seems conveniently irrelevant.

A great many of the conspiracy theories seem to gain momentum and supposed 'detail' as time passes, in just the same way as Dorothy Seekings' account of the mass graves dug in rural Devon, gained additional 'detail' with every telling. What seems to escape the minds of the theorists is that none of their suppositions matter, without real concrete evidence to support them. Many of the theories and stories amount to little more than someone—usually a 'historian'—re-hashing the story from a supposedly new perspective, perhaps trying to analyse the same old documents, but in a different light and then coming to a new and more 'shocking' conclusion than the previous protagonist, who had been writing on exactly the same subject, using—more often than not—almost exactly the same 'evidence'.

Exercise Tiger is one of those events in history where, because it happened on the doorstep of something momentous and world-changing—namely D-Day, with its inherent mystery and secrecy—those who wish to seek out conspiracies will always manage to find them. Unfortunately these theories can then be published and, because there are a great many publishers who no longer know how to (or bother to) edit their titles, or because the author can easily self-publish, that theory may soon gain some rather dubious credence and start to become accepted as a new version of the truth and its creator as an authority on the subject, simply because his or her words are in print.

There are several writers, enthusiasts and so-called 'historians' who propound a great many theories regarding the E-boat attack of Exercise Tiger and its aftermath. The information for some of these theories comes from first-hand accounts, letters and diaries, which might be assumed to the reading public to make them accurate. However, as has already been shown elsewhere in this chapter, this is not necessarily the case and, regardless of accuracy, the 'evidence' used will always depend upon the reliability and possibly any agenda of the source. If someone has a particular axe to grind, their perspective may be necessarily skewed.

There are some, for example, who will always decry the casualty figures of either 639 or 749 as an under-estimate, believing that this number has been deliberately massaged downwards by the US government and/or military. Quite often, however, the only reason given for this is someone's recollection of there having been 'hundreds' of men in the water, or on the tank deck, or that there were 'dozens' of trucks on the beach waiting to remove the bodies. Such memories are vague and individual and, quite often, contradicted by evidence offered from another source. At the same time, the theorists can usually provide no valid reason as to why the authorities would have wanted to instigate a cover-up, other than the fact that this is what governments do—evidently.

It has been claimed that some of the official reports and logs, such as the one given by Lieutenant James Murdock (the senior surviving officer on LST-507) were 'doctored', or that Murdock was ordered to fabricate his answers in his interview to conceal the true number of casualties and sequence of events. This accusation has not only been applied to Murdock, but to others who were supposedly forced to change their version of events in a supposedly enormous cover-up. The evidence for these accusations would appear to be that some of these reports, from different people, are too similar to each other, which would seem to suggest that the writers have been influenced by someone outside and instructed as to what they should say, or that reports have been re-written, after their first draft. Senior naval officers are accused, by conspiracy theorists, of dashing around all over the countryside to 'get to' various members of the crews of the LSTs, so that they could be given the 'official' version of the event, which they were then permitted to reveal when questioned. This effort of influencing the senior participants is even alleged to have extended to the Royal Navy, in the form of Lieutenant-Commander Geddes, who was supposedly convinced to lie on behalf of the US Navy and state that his vessel had not stopped to pick up any survivors, when—the theorists propound—it really had done so. The basis for this last and, frankly ludicrous, accusation, is the word of one survivor, who claims to have been rescued by Geddes' ship, HMS *Azalea*. It must be said, however, that this same witness and survivor also claims that there were six—not two—LSTs that were sunk during the E-boat attack and that the 'concealment' of this fact is also part of the US military and government cover-up.

The theorists argue that, because Lieutenant Murdock and Ensign Harlander used similar language in their accounts of the event, they must, therefore, have been coached as to what they should say when questioned. It seems impossible, somehow, for them to believe that two men, who had gone through the same, or similar, experiences might use the same, or similar, words to describe events.

At the same time as making these more personal accusations and suggestions, the number of casualties is also often called into question, with estimates sometimes rising into the thousands. These calculations are based on hearsay and unsubstantiated reports of loading figures having been tampered with at some stage after the event. However, once again, these suppositions do not really bear scrutiny. For example, in recent years, the muster rolls for the LSTs—clearly original and with no alterations—have become available, showing that quite a few men were transferred off of the vessels on the day of embarkation, or just before. It seems quite unlikely that, having kept such meticulous records of the movements of each individual, the US Navy would then mistakenly—or even deliberately—'lose' a few hundred men, for no apparently justified reason. Nonetheless, because there is now really no absolute and definitive way of proving precisely how many men died that night and because some of the friendly fire casualties from the previous day may have become included in the overall 'official' death toll of 749 from the E-boat attack, there must, therefore have been a government-led cover-up instigated at the time for purely monstrous purposes, which bore no relation whatsoever to the impending D-Day landings, or the need for secrecy which surrounded and accompanied them.

As well as the casualty figures, the other, more general aspect of Exercise Tiger which has been called into question, is the treatment of the bodies of the victims. This has clearly been based upon and given credence by the stories told by Dorothy Seekings, whose versions of events surrounding mass burials are deemed by some to be true, evidently for the simple reason that her story has appeared in a local newspaper. These accounts have gone on to become the basis for yet another conspiracy theory, based around the burials at Brookwood Cemetery in Surrey, which are supposed to also have been part of the great 'cover-up'. It is assumed that the bodies were too numerous to transport to Brookwood, so some had to be buried locally (as Mrs Seekings reported). The Brookwood bodies were then disinterred and moved to Cambridge, along with those buried in the mass graves in Devon. Having visited Brookwood Cemetery myself and spent a considerable time speaking to the curator and representative of the American Battle Monuments Commission, I have been able to verify that, while the Exercise Tiger Casualties were all moved from Brookwood—either to be repatriated at the request of their families or to be reinterred at Cambridge—there was never any question at the time that they were all buried properly. However, according to the conspiracy theorists, the need to hide the 'truth' regarding the whereabouts of the bodies and the casualty figures continued into the 1950s, with the manipulation of official reports regarding the repatriation and reinterment of bodies. Anyone who has had dealings with the American Battle Monuments Commission, or has visited an American military cemetery will know that there are few nations who treat there war dead with more respect and reverence than the United States. To suggest otherwise and, especially that they would simply dig a large hole in a field, fill it with bodies and just forget about it for decades, not only shows contempt for the US military, but for the country as a whole.

Perhaps—at least in my view—the most ridiculous of the many conspiratorial suggestions surrounds the suicide of Rear-Admiral Moon. It would appear, according to the theorists, that we should not believe the official version of events, that Moon was suffering from combat fatigue, nor should we pay any attention to the account of Commander John Robert Lewis Jr., who served under Rear-Admiral Moon from January 1944 and was on board USS *Bayfield* when Moon shot himself. Instead, we are supposed to believe—with no evidence to corroborate this—that Moon had threatened to expose the 'cover-up' being perpetrated and perpetuated by the US military and government and the order was given for him to be silenced, rather than allowing him to reveal their supposedly dirty secrets. The only other alternative solution offered for Moon's death, is that he was so ashamed and guilty about his own role within the evident 'cover-up' that he could no longer live with himself and decided to commit suicide.

Overall, these accusations call into question the integrity of just about everyone involved in the exercise, with the exception of those who have supplied the damning 'evidence' in the first place. They also belittle the judgment and professionalism of men whose situation we cannot hope to understand, most of whom acted with a bravery and commitment to duty to which very few of us can aspire. As with many supposed 'historians', some of these writers are very capable of 'cherry picking' their witnesses, or the sections of the eyewitness accounts which they wish to use in order to lend a little credence and realism to the telling of their story. All too often, unfortunately, this is based not on a desire to get to the truth, or tell the genuine accounts of the men who were there, but on their own desire to have their 'fifteen minutes of fame', for having arrived at a new and startling truth that everyone else has evidently missed, but which, upon closer inspection, somehow fails to deliver.

Exercise Tiger is not about sensationalism or scandal. It is not about conspiracies and cover-ups. It is, quite simply, a sad and sorry story of ordinary men, who were farmers, clerks and factory workers, truck drivers and teachers, who went to sea one day and who briefly endured the unendurable and, in doing so became, perhaps, one of the most unsung groups of extraordinary men.

'When the Lights Go On'

It seems quite remarkable, looking back, that most of the men who had survived the E-boat attack on convoy T-4 were then ordered to take part in the D-Day landings forty days later. Almost none of them were allowed any leave in between and the only men who seem to have been excused from duty were those who were too badly injured to carry on. This may be considered by some to be standard military practice in the circumstances, but it also indicates the importance of D-Day, in that no-one could be spared from duty. This requirement to continue and the lack of leave granted, certainly did not sit well with a great many of the survivors of the E-boat attack who, even many years later, still resented the treatment they were shown by the authorities. It is all too easy to forget, in today's climate, when our armed forces are comprised of professional soldiers, sailors, marines and airmen, that these servicemen, who fought in the Second World War, were really civilians, who had been given a uniform, handed a gun and—all too often—woefully inadequate training, before being ordered to do a soldier's job.

One of the unknown statistics is how many of the survivors of Exercise Tiger went on to perish in the Normandy Landings. One can easily believe that, despite their indignation over their treatment, these veterans would have heaved a sigh of relief, thinking that the E-boat attack had afforded them their share of bad luck, but D-Day and the push through the occupied European territories cost many more lives, making it perfectly possible that some of those who lost their lives between 6 June 1944 and the end of the war, might also have been survivors of the E-boat attack of 28 April.

Lessons were undoubtedly learned as a result of the many exercises that were carried out in the build-up to D-Day—not just the costly E-boat attack of Exercise Tiger—but all of the practice exercises that preceded it. These lessons may well have helped to limit the number of casualties on Utah Beach during the Normandy Landings.

The fact of the E-boat attack having taken place is really just a small part of the whole story, in which over a million men were prepared for the biggest and most important battle of the Second World War. The arrival of the E-boats on the scene was no-one's fault. It was one of those unfortunate circumstances, the like of which simply occur during wars. The immediate aftermath of the attack is a different matter, however. One has to question, for example, why and how Commander Skahill on board LST-*515* did not realise that the attack was genuine upon first sighting a burning vessel in the water. His failure to act quickly and decisively proved costly and even if he believed that this was only a part of the exercise, to take no action at all seems lamentably poor. Equally, the failure of Skahill and Lieutenant-Commander Geddes to arrange any form of communication prior to the event, or of any of their senior officers to ensure this was done, was a pivotal error in managing the convoy and its escort, for which those involved would pay heavily. At the same time, there were other catastrophes, such as the delay in sending out a replacement escort vessel when HMS *Scimitar* was recalled to Plymouth. Caused by another shortcoming in communications, this failure to act in a more timely fashion meant that there was no second escort vessel on hand. To have a destroyer close to the convoy when the E-boats struck might well have afforded the LSTs more protection and could have resulted in a greater number of men being rescued. The delay in the arrival of HMS *Saladin* and the other Royal Navy ships in the area, meant that the men in the water stood much less chance of survival in the icy waters.

On a more personal level, it became clear after the event, that a great many of the men involved—especially the army personnel—had not received sufficient training in what to do if and when a ship on which they were travelling hit trouble. They were being trained in how to carry out an amphibious landing, but not in how to deal with the consequences of being on board a vessel that came under attack. Hence most of the army personnel had no idea how to use an inflatable life belt, resulting in numerous unnecessary deaths through drowning.

These are just a few examples of the lessons that were learned as a result of the E-boat attack and do not take into account the many additional issues which had arisen from the earlier exercises, most of which were acted upon prior to the D-Day landings. Despite the heavy cost, there was a purpose.

There was one lesson, however, which everyone failed to learn and which continues to afflict the soldiers, sailors, marines and airmen of today's armed forces. That lesson takes us right back to where this story first began, with a few men in suits, sitting in a conference room, discussing the course of a war, from a remote and safe distance. It remains a sorry and eternal truth, from which men never seem to learn anything, that, while politicians and leaders might create wars, it falls to better and braver men than them to fight and die. Sometimes the cause might be worth it—depending upon one's viewpoint—but sometimes, as happened in Exercise Tiger, the cause for which they give their lives, seems too senseless for words.

'The Army, The Navy and The Air Force'

A Who's Who of military personnel involved in Exercise Tiger

Captain James Arnold (USN): Naval Officer in Command for Utah Beach Landings

Major General Ray Barker (US Army): Deputy Chief of Staff for Supreme Headquarters Allied Expeditionary Force

Major-General Raymond O. Barton (US Army): Fourth Infantry Division

Lieutenant John W. Behrens (USNR): Commanding Officer LST-*531*

Rear-Admiral Bernhard Bieri (USN): Naval Adviser to the Supreme Commander, attached to the Staff of Rear-Admiral Sir Bertram Ramsay (RN)

General Omar Bradley (US Army): Commander US Army, North-West Europe

Rear-Admiral E. J. P. Brind (RN): Assistant Chief of Naval Staff, Home

General Sir Alan Brooke (British Army): Chief of the Imperial General Staff

Captain Harry Butcher (US Army): Aide to General Eisenhower

Colonel Eugene Caffey (US Army): Commander, 1st Engineer Special Brigade

Admiral Wilhelm Franz Canaris (Abwehr—German Military Intelligence): Head of Abwehr

General Joseph Lawton Collins (US Army): Commander, US 7th Corps

Rear-Admiral Charles M. Cooke (USN): US Navy Chief of Planning

Major-General Charles H. Corlett (US Army): Commander XIX Corps

General Henry D. G. "Harry" Crerar (Canadian Army): Commanding Officer, 1st Canadian Army

Second Coxswain John Cullen: HMRML *532*

General Miles Dempsey (British Army): Commander British 2nd Army

Lieutenant John Doyle (USN): Commander LST-*515*

Brigadier General Dwight D. Eisenhower (US Army): Supreme Allied Commander

Captain J. P. Farquharson (RN): Commanding Officer, HMS *Attack*, Portland

Lord Fortescue: Lord-Lieutenant of Devon

Lieutenant Commander George C. Geddes (RNR): Captain, HMS *Azalea*

General Leonard T. Gerow (US Army): Commander V Corps

Oberleutnant zur See Götschke (German Navy): Commander S-*140*

Rear-Admiral John L. Hall Jnr. (USN): Naval Commander "Force O" (Omaha)

Lieutenant Moses Hallett: Communications Officer, T-4

Air Marshall Arthur Harris (RAF): Marshal of the Royal Air Force

Major-General Clarence R. Huebner (US Army): Commander 1st Infantry Division

Major Ralph Ingersoll (US Army): American liaison officer on General Montgomery's staff

Major-General Sir Hastings Ismay (British Army): Prime Minister's Chief of Staff and Deputy Secretary to the War Cabinet

Kapitänleutnant Jurgenmeyer (German Navy): Captain of S-*136*

Admiral Ernest J. King (USN): Chief of Naval Operations

Lieutenant-Commander Philip Geoffrey Colet King (RNVR): Commander, HMS *Saladin*

Rear-Admiral Alan Kirk (USN): Commander Western Naval Task Force

Korvettenkapitän Bernd Klug (German Navy): Chief of 5th S-Boot (E-Boat) Flotilla

Lieutenant Stanley Koch (USNR): Commander LST-*496*

Admiral Theodor Krancke (German Navy): Commander-in-Chief of Navy Group Command West

Rear-Admiral Sir Ralph Leatham (RN): British Naval Commander in Chief, Plymouth

Air Chief Marshal Sir Trafford Leigh-Mallory (RAF): British Tactical Air Commander

Vice-Admiral Charles Little (RN): British Naval Commander in Chief, Portsmouth

Brigadier-General Anthony McAuliffe (US Army): Commander of Artillery for 101st Airborne Division

General George C. Marshall (US Army): US Army Chief of Staff

Lieutenant Harry Mettler (USNR): Commanding Officer LST-*289*

Major-General Henry J. F. Miller (USAAF): Chief Supply Officer of the US 9th Air Force and BIGOT

1st Viscount Bernard Montgomery of Alamein (British Army): Commander 21st Army Group

Rear-Admiral Don P. Moon (USN): Naval Commander "Force U" (Utah) and in charge of "Exercise Tiger"

Commander John Moreno (USN): Air and Assistant Plans Officer on Rear-Admiral Moon's Staff, based on HMS *Bayfield* during Exercise Tiger

Lieutenant-General Frederick Morgan (British Army): Commander British 1 Corps and initial COSSAG (Chief of Staff, Supreme Allied Commander—designate) of Operation Overlord

Rear-Admiral Llewellyn V. Morgan (RN): Director of Signal Division

Vice-Admiral Lord Louis Mountbatten (RN): Chief of Combined Operations Headquarters

Lieutenant-General Sir Archibald Nye (British Army): Vice Chief of the Imperial General Staff

Lieutenant-General George S Patton (US Army): Commander Third US Army

Kapitän zur See Rudolf Peterson (German Navy): Commander of E-boats

Commander J. L. Phares (USN): Commander USS *Augusta*

Oberleutnant zur See Gunter Rabe (German Navy): Captain of S-*130*

Rear-Admiral Sir Bertram Ramsay (RN): Allied Naval Commander, Expeditionary Force

Colonel Ralph Rayner: MP for Totnes, Devon

Colonel A. B. Renshaw (US Army): US Defence Attaché

Captain M. T. Richardson (US Navy): Second in Command to Rear-Admiral Moon

Field-Marshal Erwin Rommel (German Army): Commander German Forces,
 Normandy
General Theodore Roosevelt (US Army): Deputy Commander Fourth Infantry
 Division
Commander Scott: Captain HMRML *532*
Captain Ray Seibert (557th QM RH Co): Senior Army Officer aboard LST-*507*
Lieutenant Philip Archer Shee (RNR): Commanding Officer, HMS *Scimitar*
Commander Bernard Joseph Skahill (USN): Commodore of T-4
General Walter Bedell Smith (US Army): Chief of Staff to General Eisenhower
General Carl Spaatz (USAF): Chief of Staff of the United States Air Force
Captain Lyndon Spencer (USCG): Commander USS *Bayfield*
Admiral Harold R. Stark (USN): Commander of American Naval Forces in
 European Waters
Oberleutnant zur See Stehwasser (German Navy): Captain of S-*138*
Rear-Admiral Arthur Struble (USN): Chief of Staff to Rear-Admiral Kirk
Lieutenant James S. Swarts (USNR): Commanding Officer, LST-*507*
Major-General Maxwell D. Taylor (US Army): Commander 101st Airborne Division
Air Chief Marshal Sir Arthur Tedder (RAF): Deputy Supreme Commander
Commander Robert H. Thayer (USN): Intelligence Officer to Rear-Admiral Moon
Captain Tompkins (USN): Chief of Staff to Admiral Moon
Lieutenant-Commander Harold Unwin, DSC (RN): Commander HMS *Obedient*
Kapitänleutnant Freiherr Von Mirbach (German Navy): Chief of 9th Schnellboote
 Flotilla
Field-Marshal Gerd von Rundstedt (German Army): Commander German Forces in
 the West
Lieutenant John Wachter (USN): Commanding Officer, LST-*58*
Rear-Admiral John Wilkes (USN): Commander Landing Craft and Bases,
 Amphibious Forces, Europe
Lieutenant John Yacevich (USN): Commander LST-*511*

Roll of Honour

Abbreviations

Ranks:

Cl. - Class; Co. - Company; Hosp. - Hospital; JG - Junior Grade; Mach. - Machinist(s); Pharm. - Pharmacist(s); QM - Quartermaster.

Units:

Amph. - Amphibious; Bn. - Battalion; CM Decon. - Chemical Decontamination; Co. - Company; Hosp. - Hospital; Pharm. - Pharmacist(s); QM - Quartermaster; RH - Railhead.

Decoration:

BS - Bronze Star; PH - Purple Heart; PH+OLC - Purple Heart with Oak Leaf Clusters; SS - Silver Star.

USS LST-289
US Navy

Last	First	Middle	Rank	Unit	Decoration
Broske	Mitchell	Louis	Gunners Mate 3rd Cl.	US Navy	
Chandler	James	William	Gunners Mate 2nd Cl.	US Navy	SS, PH
Frazier	Walter	Humphris	Seaman, 2nd Cl.	US Naval Reserve	
Griffin	Joseph	William	Storekeeper, 2nd Cl.	US Naval Reserve	
Hackes	Mike	George	Seaman, 2nd Cl.	US Naval Reserve	PH
Harvie	James	Hugh	Seaman, 2nd Cl.	US Naval Reserve	
Kortenhorn	Herman	Russell	Fireman, 1st Cl.	US Navy	
May	Robert	M			
Muller	William	Carl	Seaman, 2nd Cl.	US Naval Reserve	
Muza	Earl	Valentine	Seaman, 2nd Cl.	US Naval Reserve	
Neff	Harold	Albert	Seaman, 2nd Cl.	US Naval Reserve	
Roberts	Clifford	Laverne	QM, 3rd Cl.	US Naval Reserve	
Shipp	John Jr	Lewis	Seaman, 1st Cl.	US Naval Reserve	

USS LST-507
US Army

Last	First	Middle	Rank	Unit	Decoration
Alexander	Walter	W	Private	557th RH Co.	PH
Allen	John	J	Technician 5th Cl.	478th Amph. Truck Co.	PH
Arcuri	Sam	S	Technician 5th Cl.	478th Amph. Truck Co.	
Barrett	Chester		Staff Sergeant	557th RH Co.	PH
Battle	William	Russell	Private	557th QM RH Co.	PH
Bernardo	John			33 CM Decon. Co.	
Bertini	Nilo	V	Private 1st Cl.	33 CM Decon. Co.	PH
Blake	Floyd	E	Technician 4th Cl.	557th QM RH Co.	
Blind	Frederick	W	Private	478th Amph. Truck Co.	PH
Blond	William		Private	557th QM RH Co.	
Bohl	Jacob	A	Private	557th QM RH Co.	PH
Brown	Edward	L	Private	306th QM Bn, 557th QM RH Co.	PH
Brown	George	E	Technician 5th Cl.	557th RH Co.	PH
Brown	John	B	Private	478th Amph. Truck Co.	
Brumfield	John	W	Private	33 CM Decon. Co.	PH
Campbell	Terrence Jr	V	Private	306th QM Bn, 557th QM RH Co.	PH
Campbell	William	M	Private 1st Cl.	557th RH Co.	PH
Catman	Ulysses	J	Private	478th Amph. Truck Co.	
Cavanaugh	James	P	Private	557th QM RH Co.	
Clayton	Kenneth			33 CM Decon. Co.	
Coleman	Guy		Private 1st Cl.	306th QM Bn, 557th QM RH Co.	PH
Conner	Willie	J	Private	306th QM Bn, 557th QM RH Co.	PH
Cooke	Robert	M	Private	478th Amph. Truck Co.	PH
Craig	Arthur	L	Private	557th QM RH Co.	PH
Crawford	Poindexter Jr	D	Private 1st Cl.	557th QM RH Co.	PH
Cutrone	Samuel	J	Technician 5th Cl.	478th Amph. Truck Co.	PH
Deakyne	Clarence Jr	O	Staff Sergeant	33 CM Decon. Co.	PH
Di Pasquale	Michael		2nd Lieutenant	557th RH Co.	PH
Dindino	Paul	J	Technician 5th Cl.	478th Amph. Truck Co.	PH+OLC
Dobson	Troy		Private 1st Cl.	605th QM Bn, 557th QM RH Co.	PH
Dubisz	Frank		Private 1st Cl.	478th Amph. Truck Co.	PH
Dye	Quong	J	Private 1st Cl.	557th QM RH Co.	
Eintracht	Herman		Private	557th QM RH Co.	PH
Fischer	Edwin	G	Private	306th QM Bn, 557th QM RH Co.	PH
Fleming	Herman		Technician 5th Cl.	478th Amph. Truck Co.	PH
Follmer	William	J	Private 1st Cl.	557th RH Co.	PH
Glass	John	P	Technician 5th Cl.	557th QM RH Co.	
Godsey	Shirley	Charles	Technician 5th Cl.	557th QM RH Co.	PH
Gonshirski	John	J	Private	557th QM RH Co.	
Grigsby	Roy	B	Private	478th Amph. Truck Co.	PH
Grossman	Harold	H	Technician 5th Cl.	478th Amph. Truck Co.	PH
Hanks	John	P	Private 1st Cl.	557th QM RH Co.	
Haynes	Ernest	P	Private	557th QM RH Co.	
Hogland	Alvie	M	Private 1st Cl.	557th QM RH Co.	
Hoops	George	E	Private	1605th Map Section	
Humble	Merle	B	Technician 5th Cl.	478th Amph. Truck Co.	

Johnson	John	T	Corporal	306th QM Bn, 557th QM RH Co.	PH
Johnson	Horace		Private	33 CM Decon. Co.	PH
Johnston	Claude	E	Private 1st Cl.	306th QM Bn, 557th QM RH Co.	PH
Joyal	Raymond	O	Technician 5th Cl.	478th Amph. Truck Co.	PH
Knight	Elmer	L	Private 1st Cl.	557th QM RH Co.	PH
Lambert	Douglas	L	Private 1st Cl.	557th QM RH Co.	
Lee	Harold	E	Technician 4th Cl.	478th Amph. Truck Co.	PH
Lo Presto	Joseph Jr	P	Private 1st Cl.	306th QM Bn, 557th QM RH Co.	PH
Mancuso	Joseph	P	Technician 5th Cl.	478th Amph. Truck Co.	PH
Marcum	Glenn	R	Private	557th RH Co.	PH
Marino	Joseph	A	Private	557th RH Co.	PH
Marino	Patty		Private 1st Cl.	557th QM RH Co.	
Marts	Wilbur		Private 1st Cl.	306th QM Bn, 557th QM RH Co.	PH
Massa	Charles	F	Private 1st Cl.	478th Amph. Truck Co.	PH
Methner	Paul	H	Private 1st Cl.	557th RH Co.	PH
Mieczkowski	Harry		Technician 5th Cl.	33 CM Decon. Co.	
Miglianico	John	A		478th Amph. Truck Co.	
Misciagno	Christian		Technician 5th Cl.	3891st QM Truck Co.	PH
Mitchell	James	Charles	Staff Sergeant	557th QM RH Co.	
Mlakar	Albert		Staff Sergeant	478th Amph. Truck Co.	
Molander	Norman	C	Private 1st Cl.	306th QM Bn, 557th QM RH Co.	PH
Monk	Clarence		Private 1st Cl.	557th RH Co.	PH
Morang	Robert	C	Private 1st Cl.	557th QM RH Co.	
Morgenstern	Aloysius	G	Private 1st Cl.	557th QM RH Co.	PH
Morse	Erwin	F	Private 1st Cl.	557th RH Co.	PH
Motley	Robert	P	Private	557th QM RH Co.	PH
Murphey	Raymond	J	Corporal	306th QM Bn, 556th QM RH Co.	PH
Music	James	E	Private 1st Cl.	306th QM Bn, 557th QM RH Co.	PH
Nathan	Hyman		Private	557th RH Co.	PH
Noel	Joseph	L	Private	306th QM Bn, 557th QM RH Co.	PH
Occhipinti	Joseph		Private	557th RH Co.	PH
Ogurek	Michael	A	Corporal	478th Amph. Truck Co.	PH
Olsen	John	A	Private 1st Cl.	557th RH Co.	PH
Panek	Helmer	E	Private 1st Cl.	33 CM Decon. Co.	PH
Parisi	Frank Jr		Private 1st Cl.	306th QM Bn, 557th QM RH Co.	PH
Pemberton	Leray		Private	306th QM Bn, 557th QM RH Co.	PH
Powell	Herrel	K	1st Lieutenant	478th Amph. Truck Co.	PH
Pritchard	Clyde	C	Technician 5th Cl.	24th Amph. Truck Bn (478th Amph. Truck Co.)	PH
Pritt	Isaac	W	Private 1st Cl.	557th QM RH Co.	
Recchione	Quirino	A	Technician 4th Cl.	33 CM Decon. Co.	PH
Reibel	Thomas	C	Private	24th Amph. Truck Bn (478th Amph. Truck Co.)	PH
Roberts	Lewis		Private	306th QM Bn, 557th QM RH Co.	PH

Rosiek	Joseph	A	Corporal	33 CM Decon. Co.	PH
Rosowski	Anthony	J	Private	33 CM Decon. Co.	
Ruoto	Victor	P	Private	306th QM Bn, 557th QM RH Co.	PH
Scanlon	Edward	T		478th Amph. Truck Co.	
Schwartz	Stephen	G	Private 1st Cl.	557th QM RH Co.	
Schwechheimer	Conrad		Private 1st Cl.	306th QM Bn, 557th QM RH Co.	PH
Seibert	Ray	E	Captain	557th QM RH Co.	
Sheridan	James	P	Technician 5th Cl.	33 CM Decon. Co.	PH
Sigman	Charles	W	Private	33 CM Decon. Co.	
Silversmith	Samuel		Private	557th QM RH Co.	
Southcott	Herbert	A	Technician 5th Cl.	478th Amph. Truck Co.	
Spitler	George	E	1st Sergeant	33 CM Decon. Co.	PH
Stokes	Horace	A		33 CM Decon. Co.	
Strapp	John	W	Technician 4th Cl.	33 CM Decon. Co.	
Strubel	Mathew	E	1st Lieutenant	306th QM Battalioin, 557th QM RH Co.	PH
Suesse	Ralph	A	Captain	33 CM Decon. Co.	PH
Swanson	Richard	E	Technical Sergeant	1605th Map Section	
Tomberlin	Clarence	H	1st Lieutenant	557th QM RH Co.	
Tuma	James Jr	L	1st Lieutenant	557th RH Co.	PH
Tyson	Ernest		Private	557th QM RH Co.	
Unger	Edward	J	Technician 5th Cl.	24th Amph. Truck Bn (478th Amph. Truck Co.)	PH
Veenbaas	John	D	Private	557th RH Co.	PH
Vieira	Manuel Jr		Private	557th QM RH Co.	
Von Wald	Richard	F	Staff Sergeant	557th RH Co.	PH
Voorhees	Harold		Corporal	306th QM Bn, 557th QM RH Co.	PH
Walsh	Joseph	J		1605th Map Section	
Welch	Elmer	O	Technician 5th Cl.	478th Amph. Truck Co.	PH
West	Chalcie	G	Private	557th QM RH Co.	
Willis	Obie	D	Technician 4th Cl.	557th QM RH Co.	
Wood	Stanley	K	Private 1st Cl.	33 CM Decon. Co.	PH
Wright	Joseph	O	Private	557th RH Co.	PH
Yangrello	Dominick			557th QM RH Co.	
Zempel	Lawrence	C	Private 1st Cl.	557th QM RH Co.	PH

US Navy

Last	First	Middle	Rank	Unit	Decoration
Bailey	James				
Bennen	Charles	D			
Bettencourt	John	J	Motor Mach.	US Naval Reserve	
Blackie	Henry	Allen	Seaman, 2nd Cl.	US Naval Reserve	
Burns	Sylvester	Michael	Electricians Mate 3rd Cl.	US Naval Reserve	PH
Cieary	James	F			
Clark	James	J	Ensign	US Naval Reserve	
Collins	Conner	D	Ensign	US Naval Reserve	
Crowe	James Jr	Thornton	Motor Mach.	US Naval Reserve	
Cusak	Vincent	P			
Daily	Carl	W	Pharm.	US Naval Reserve	
Del Duca	Thomas Jr	J			
Dickerson	William	Wesley	Storekeeper, 2nd Cl.		

Dinneen	Joseph	M	Boatswains Mate, 1st Cl.	US Naval Reserve	
Dobson	Henry	R	Pharm. Mate 2nd Cl.	US Naval Reserve	
Durrum	James	William	Seaman, 1st Cl.	US Naval Reserve	
Eisenbach	Harold	Edwin	Ship	US Naval Reserve	
Field	Paul	Robert	QM, 3rd Cl.	US Navy	
Fitts	Felton	Thomas	Gunner	US Navy	
Gambrel	Jake		Seaman, 2nd Cl.	US Naval Reserve	PH
Garlock	Charles	W	QM, 2nd Cl.	US Naval Reserve	
Geehan	Raymond	Richard	Gunner	US Naval Reserve	
Gibson	Richard	Moulton	Seaman, 1st Cl.	US Naval Reserve	
Goldsmith	Leonard		Seaman, 2nd Cl.	US Naval Reserve	
Grecco	Joseph	Gabriel	Radioman, 3rd Cl.	US Naval Reserve	
Griffin	Jimmie	Wallace		US Naval Reserve	
Grunther	Nelson		Signalman, 3rd Cl.	US Naval Reserve	PH
Gulledge	William	Thomas	Seaman, 2nd Cl.	US Naval Reserve	
Hampton	Jerry	Proffit	Seaman, 1st Cl.	US Naval Reserve	
Hoffman	Russel	Wagner	Seaman, 1st Cl.	US Navy	
Hofmann	Bruce	Brunner	Lieutenant, JG	US Naval Reserve	BS, PH
Karasinski	Louis	Francis	Seaman, 1st Cl.	US Naval Reserve	
King	Philip	Edward	Fireman, 2nd Cl.	US Naval Reserve	
Koski	Theodore	J	Motor Mach.	US Naval Reserve	
Ledbetter	Alvin	Lee	Seaman, 2nd Cl.	US Naval Reserve	
Lichty	Frank Jr	Titus	Motor Mach. Mate	US Naval Reserve	PH
Mackey	Robert	Clyde	Coxswain	US Naval Reserve	
Maggard	Daniel Jr	Willard	Seaman, 2nd Cl.	US Naval Reserve	
Malott	Robert	Joseph	Pharm.	US Naval Reserve	
Martin	Howard	Abraham	Seaman, 2nd Cl.	US Naval Reserve	
Mathews	John	E	Seaman, 2nd Cl.	US Naval Reserve	
Miller	John	H	Seaman, 2nd Cl.	US Naval Reserve	
Moore	Joseph	Martin	Seaman, 2nd Cl.	US Naval Reserve	
Morancy	Edgar	Freeman	Seaman, 2nd Cl.	US Naval Reserve	
Myers	Lester	Atlee	Fireman, 2nd Cl.	US Naval Reserve	
O'Connell	Michael	Joseph	Motor Mach.	US Naval Reserve	
Ragusa	Paul	Martin	Pharm. Mate, 3rd Cl.	US Naval Reserve	PH
Raptis	Charles	George	Pharm.	US Naval Reserve	
Ricketts	Richard	Earl	Hosp. Apprentice 2nd Cl.	US Naval Reserve	
Rogers	William	L	Hosp. Apprentice 2nd Cl.	US Naval Reserve	
Ryan	James Jr	P	Signalman, 3rd Cl.	US Naval Reserve	
Saucier	Henry	Quitman	Lieutenant, JG	US Naval Reserve	
Saxton	Robert	Earl	Hosp. Apprentice 2nd Cl.	US Naval Reserve	PH
Schreiber	William	Henry	Seaman, 2nd Cl.	US Naval Reserve	
Scott	Kenneth	Lutz	Hosp. Apprentice 2nd Cl.	US Naval Reserve	PH
Smith	Kennan	Hoff	Lieutenant	US Naval Reserve	
Squiers	Lawrence	Perry	Motor Mach.	US Naval Reserve	
Stanesic	John	Lawrence	Hosp. Apprentice 2nd Cl.	US Naval Reserve	
Staudt	Charles Jr	J	Motor Mach. Mate	US Naval Reserve	PH
Sturdivant	Malcolm	Eugene	Water Tender, 2nd Cl.	US Navy	PH
Sullivan	George	Alexander	Seaman, 2nd Cl.	US Naval Reserve	
Sutherland	Pete	J	Seaman, 2nd Cl.	US Naval Reserve	

Swartz	James	Strickland	Lieutenant	US Naval Reserve	
Trgovic	Steve	J			
Tully	Joseph	Edward	Hosp. Apprentice 2nd Cl.	US Naval Reserve	PH
Watson	Andrew		Motor Mach. Mate	US Naval Reserve	PH
Weinbrot	Harold	Murry	Hosp. Apprentice 1st Cl.	US Naval Reserve	
Whipple	Frank	Leslie	Seaman, 2nd Cl.	US Naval Reserve	
Woods	Deward	Woodrow	Gunner	US Navy	
Wright	Curtis	Milton	Hosp. Apprentice 2nd Cl.	US Naval Reserve	

USS LST-531
US Army

Last	First	Middle	Rank	Unit	Decoration
Adcock	Ovid	C	Private	3206th QM Service Co.	PH
Aid	Alvin	E	Private 1st Cl.	3206th QM Service Co.	PH
Alexander	Marvin	R	Private 1st Cl.	607th Graves Registration Co.	PH
Allen	Delmar	R	Corporal	3206th QM Service Co.	PH
Alsip	Albert	F	Technician 5th Cl.	24th Amph. Truck Bn (462nd Amph. Truck Co.)	PH
Arismendiz	Joe	M	Private 1st Cl.	3206th QM Service Co.	PH
Asberry	Marion	J	Private	3206th QM Service Co.	PH
Augustynski	William		Private 1st Cl.	35th Signal Construction Bn	PH
Baldwin	Raymond		Private	3206th QM Service Co.	PH
Banister	Calvin	C	Sergeant	3206th QM Service Co.	PH
Barber	Ralph	E	Private	3206th QM Service Co.	PH
Barber	John	L	Private	56th General Hosp.	
Basgall	Edwin	A	Private 1st Cl.	3206th QM Service Co.	PH
Baugus	James	R	Private	3206th QM Service Co.	PH
Bean	Carl	M	Private 1st Cl.	625th Ordnance Ammunition Co.	PH
Bergfeld	Walter	B		3206th QM Service Co.	
Bird	Howard	G	Private	3206th QM Service Co.	PH
Birkley	Louis Jr	L	Private	3206th QM Service Co.	PH
Bisaillon	Martial	J	Technician 5th Cl.	531st Engineer Shore Regt.	PH
Blethroad	Thomas	J	Private 1st Cl.	3206th QM Service Co.	PH
Blevins	Harley	E	Private 1st Cl.	3206th QM Service Co.	PH
Bolton	Louis	Archer	Sergeant	607th Graves Registration Co.	PH
Bonderer	Bernard	E	Corporal	3206th QM Service Co.	PH
Borchers	Harvey	J	Private 1st Cl.	531st Engineer Shore Regt.	PH
Bost	Winford	G	Private	3206th QM Service Co.	PH
Boyles	Hoy	F	Private	3206th QM Service Co.	
Bratton	Portter	J	Private	3206th QM Service Co.	PH
Brewer	Wayne	R	Private 1st Cl.	531st Engineer Shore Regt.	PH
Brown	Ivan	J	Private	3206th QM Service Co.	PH
Bryant	Donald	S	Private 1st Cl.	531st Engineer Shore Regt.	
Bryson	Ernest	C	Private	3206th QM Service Co.	
Buckner	George	W	Private 1st Cl.	3206th QM Service Co.	PH

Burke	Robert	E	Private 1st Cl.	3206th QM Service Co.	PH
Burks	Floyd	H	Private	3206th QM Service Co.	PH
Burns	Harold	W	Private	3206th QM Service Co.	PH
Burrell	Robert	T	Private 1st Cl.	3206th QM Service Co.	PH
Butry	Metro		Private	3206th QM Service Co.	PH
Cain	Jay	H	Corporal	3206th QM Service Co.	PH
Caldwell	Paul Jr		Private	3206th QM Service Co.	PH
Callahan	John	H	Private 1st Cl.	3206th QM Service Co.	PH
Caracciolo	Dominick		Private 1st Cl.	607th Graves Registration Co.	
Carey	Ernest		Private	3206th QM Service Co.	PH
Cates	Georgie		Private	3206th QM Service Co.	PH
Cesaro	Libro	Charles	Private	3206th QM Service Co.	PH
Chamberlain	Richard		Private	3206th QM Service Co.	PH
Chambers	Robert	G	Private	3206th QM Service Co.	
Childs	Donald	H	Staff Sergeant	3206th QM Service Co.	PH
Chudzinski	Arthur	F	Private	3206th QM Service Co.	PH
Ciccio	Joseph		Corporal	3206th QM Service Co.	PH
Circle	Ott	S	Private	3206th QM Service Co.	PH
Clardy	John	J	Technician 5th Cl.	462nd Amph. Truck Co.	PH
Clark	Herman	D	Private 1st Cl.	3206th QM Service Co.	
Coan	Francis	M	Private	3206th QM Service Co.	PH
Conklin	Robert	J	Technician 5th Cl.	462nd Amph. Truck Co.	
Constant	Woodson	Dean	Private	3206th QM Service Co.	PH
Cope	Christopher	T	Private 1st Cl.	3206th QM Service Co.	
Cottrell	James	O	Private	3206th QM Service Co.	PH
Crandell	Harold	E	Private	3206th QM Service Co.	PH
Crane	Carroll	S	Private	3206th QM Service Co.	PH
Creed	Thomas Jr	C	Corporal	3206th QM Service Co.	PH
Crocker	Ed	W	Private	3206th QM Service Co.	PH
Cruikshank	James	F	Private 1st Cl.	35th Signal Construction Bn	PH
Cutrone	Allesantro		Technician 5th Cl.	462nd Amph. Truck Co.	PH
Czyzniak	Stephen	J	Technician 5th Cl.	462nd Amph. Truck Co.	PH
Dakis	Nick	G	Private	607th Graves Registration Co.	PH
Dame	Homer	L	Corporal	3206th QM Service Co.	PH
Daniels	Leroy		Private	518th Port Bn	
Danner	Fred	S	Private 1st Cl.	3206th QM Service Co.	PH
Daoukas	Thomas		Private 1st Cl.	3206th QM Service Co.	PH
Davenport	Bernard	A	Sergeant	478th Amph. Truck Co.	PH
Davis	Franklin Jr	W	Private 1st Cl.	3207th QM Service Co.	PH
De Baene	Morris	J	Corporal	3206th QM Service Co.	PH
De Hass	Paul Jr	R	Sergeant	3206th QM Service Co.	PH
De Salvo	Joseph	F	Technician 5th Cl.	3206th QM Service Co.	PH
Delamater	Edward	J	1st Lieutenant	607th Graves Registration Co.	PH
DeLeon	Anastacio		Private 1st Cl.	556th QM RH Co.	
Delitko	John	A	Private 1st Cl.	625th Ordnance Ammunition Co.	PH
Donaldson	Garland	W	Private	3206th QM Service Co.	PH
Donaldson	Alexander	G	Technician 4th Cl.	625th Ordnance Ammunition Co.	PH

Douglas	Earl	V	Private	3206th QM Service Co.	PH
Douglas	John Jr	M	Technician 5th Cl.	3206th QM Service Co.	PH
Drawdy	Oscar Jr	L	Technician 5th Cl.	462nd Amph. Truck Co.	PH
Duckworth	Meredith	J	Private 1st Cl.	3206th QM Service Co.	PH
Dunahoo	Bruce	E	Private	35th Signal Construction Bn	PH
Duncan	William	A	Private	3206th QM Service Co.	PH
Duncan	Johnnie	O	Private	3206th QM Service Co.	PH
Earnest	Ralph	T	Private	3206th QM Service Co.	PH
Eckhoff	Roy	E	Private 1st Cl.	3206th QM Service Co.	PH
Edelmann	Matthew		Private	3206th QM Service Co.	PH
Edwards	Bill	E	Private	3206th QM Service Co.	PH
Edwards	John	J	Private 1st Cl.	531st Engineer Shore Regt.	PH
Elliott	Carl	M	Private	3206th QM Service Co.	PH
Elliott	William	R	Private 1st Cl.	531st Engineer Shore Regt.	PH
Evangelist	Nicholas	J	Staff Sergeant	3206th QM Service Co.	PH
Farris	Junior	T	Private	3206th QM Service Co.	PH
Ferguson	Darrel	D	Private	3206th QM Service Co.	PH
Fizer	David	E	Private	3206th QM Service Co.	PH
Fletchall	Arthur	A	Private 1st Cl.	3206th QM Service Co.	PH
Floyd	Charles	R	Private	3206th QM Service Co.	PH
Flynt	Lawrence	R	Technician 5th Cl.	462nd Amph. Truck Co.	PH
Fond	Salvador	D	Private 1st Cl.	462nd Amph. Truck Co.	PH
Fontana	Russell		Private	462nd Amph. Truck Co.	PH
Ford	Adrian	L	Private	3206th QM Service Co.	PH
Foster	Harold	G		518th Port Bn	
Frank	Joseph Jr	H	Private	3206th QM Service Co.	PH
Franks	Richard	L	Private	625th Ordnance Ammunition Co.	
Freed	Hershel	G	Private	3206th QM Service Co.	PH
Friend	Leslie	W	Private 1st Cl.	3206th QM Service Co.	PH
Fults	Peter	L	Private 1st Cl.	4144th QM Service Co.	PH
Galluppi	Joseph	A	Private	3206th QM Service Co.	PH
Gamer	Eugene		Private 1st Cl.	462nd Amph. Truck Co.	PH
Gardner	Lester	J	Private	531st Engineer Shore Regt.	PH
Garrison	William	A	Technician 5th Cl.	462nd Amph. Truck Co.	PH
Garvin	Herbert	S	2nd Lieutenant	625th Ordnance Ammunition Co.	PH
Gasser	John	J	Private 1st Cl.	3206th QM Service Co.	PH
Gearhart	Walter	F	Corporal	625th Ordnance Ammunition Co.	PH
Gephart	Donald	E	Private 1st Cl.	3206th QM Service Co.	PH
Gieschen	Hilmer	L	Private 1st Cl.	3206th QM Service Co.	PH
Gillespie	Bill	E	Private 1st Cl.	3206th QM Service Co.	PH
Glasscock	John	W	Private	3206th QM Service Co.	PH
Glaze	Melvin	Robert	Private	3206th QM Service Co.	PH
Golfinopulos	Louis	J	Private 1st Cl.	3206th QM Service Co.	
Goodhue	Elmer	J	Corporal	389th QM Truck Co.	PH

Goss	Dennie		Private	3206th QM Service Co.	PH
Graham	Thomas Jr	D.	Technician 5th Cl.	3021st QM Bakery Co.	PH
Gray	William	H	Private	462nd Amph. Truck Co.	PH
Gray	James	P	Private 1st Cl.	3206th QM Service Co.	PH
Grevon	John	C	Staff Sergeant	607th Graves Registration Co.	PH
Grissom	Robert		Private	35th Signal Construction Co.	PH
Groves	Marvin	W	Technician 5th Cl.	3206th QM Service Co.	
Guffin	Dale	E	Corporal	3206th QM Service Co.	PH
Haile	Francis	L	Private 1st Cl.	3206th QM Service Co.	
Harrington	Ern	F	Private	3206th QM Service Co.	
Harrison	Frank Jr	G	Technician 4th Cl.	191st Ordnance Bn (625th Ordnance Amph. Co.)	PH
Hebert	Ravila		Private	607th Graves Registration Co.	PH
Heffernan	Peter	J	Private	3206th QM Service Co.	PH
Henley	Eugene	A	Private 1st Cl.	462nd Amph. Truck Co.	PH
Hobbs	Lester		Corporal	3206th QM Service Co.	PH
Hobbs	Charles	W	2nd Lieutenant	462nd Amph. Truck Co.	
Hollon	Otis	L	Private 1st Cl.	3206th QM Service Co.	
Holmes	Samuel Jr	D	Motor Mach. Mate, 2nd Cl.	US Naval Reserve	
Holmes	Robert	E	Sergeant	607th Graves Registration Co.	PH
Holzberger	Stephen Jr	G	Private 1st Cl.	462nd Amph. Truck Co.	PH
Hopkins	Robert	L	Technician 5th Cl.	3206th QM Service Co.	PH
Hovis	Albert	H	Private	3206th QM Service Co.	PH
Hudson	Francis	L C	Private 1st Cl.	3206th QM Service Co.	PH
Huelsmann	Anton		Private	607th Graves Registration Co.	PH
Humphrey	William	L	Private 1st Cl.	3206th QM Service Co.	PH
Hurt	Arnold		Private	3206th QM Service Co.	PH
Hutchison	Clifford	E	Private 1st Cl.	3206th QM Service Co.	PH
Jensen	Richard	H	Technician 5th Cl.	462nd Amph. Truck Co.	PH
Johnson	James	G	Private	462nd Amph. Truck Co.	PH
Jordan	Everett	W	Private	531st Engineer Shore Regt.	PH
Kapinos	John	A	Private	531st Engineer Shore Regt.	PH
Kay	William	M	Private 1st Cl.	3206th QM Service Co.	
Keller	Otto	W	Private 1st Cl.	3206th QM Service Co.	PH
Kielbasa	George	A	Private 1st Cl.	3206th QM Service Co.	PH
King	William	E	Private 1st Cl.	3206th QM Service Co.	PH
Kinkead	Bertran		Private 1st Cl.	3206th QM Service Co.	PH
Kladus	Johnny	D	Private	3206th QM Service Co.	PH
Klobe	John	T	Corporal	3206th QM Service Co.	
Korodi	William		Private	3206th QM Service Co.	PH
Kreiss	Ezra	F	Staff Sergeant	3206th QM Service Co.	PH
La Iacona	Salvatore		Captain	HQ, 1st Engineer Special Brigade	PH

Larson	Walter	V	Private	3206th QM Service Co.	PH
Lasswell	Clarence	E	Private 1st Cl.	3206th QM Service Co.	PH
Leach	Robert	M	Technician 5th Cl.	35th Signal Construction Bn	PH
Leishman	Robert	B	Technician 5th Cl.	462nd Amph. Truck Co.	PH
Levengood	John	E	Private	462nd Amph. Truck Co.	PH
Libla	Champ	W	Private 1st Cl.	3206th QM Service Co.	PH
Lillo	Rocco	F	Private	531st Engineer Shore Regt.	PH
Long	Evan	W	Private	3206th QM Service Co.	PH
Long	Joseph	D	Private	3206th QM Service Co.	PH
Loper	Samuel	S	Technician 5th Cl.	462nd Amph. Truck Co.	PH
Louder	Blaine	L	Private 1st Cl.	3206th QM Service Co.	
Lowell	Theodore	G	Technician 5th Cl.	531st Engineer Shore Regt.	PH
Lowrie	Earl	C	Private	3206th QM Service Co.	PH
Lutz	Otto Jr		Private	462nd Amph. Truck Co.	PH
Lyon	Wilbert	V	Private	462nd Amph. Truck Co.	PH
MacDonald	Lawrence		Staff Sergeant	3206th QM Service Co.	
Mahoney	Patrick	J	Private	3206th QM Service Co.	PH
Malassi	John		Private 1st Cl.	3206th QM Service Co.	PH
Manak	John	V	Private 1st Cl.	3206th QM Service Co.	PH
Mance	Michael		Private	306th QM Bn, 556th QM	PH
Manes	Robert	E	Private	3206th QM Service Co.	PH
Marsh	Ralph	D	Private 1st Cl.	3206th QM Service Co.	PH
Mathewson	John	I	Captain	HQ, 1st Engineer Special Briga	
Mattos	Frank	F	Technician 5th Cl.	462nd Amph. Truck Co.	PH
Mayfield	Haskel	H	Private	3206th QM Service Co.	PH
McCampbell	Louis	B	Private 1st Cl.	3206th QM Service Co.	PH
McClatchey	Evert	M	Technician 5th Cl.	35th Signal Construction Co.	PH
McCormick	Thomas	B	Sergeant	607th Graves Registration Co.	PH
McCuen	Grady	H	Private	35th Signal Construction Co.	PH
McKinnon	Roy	E	Technician 5th Cl.	3206th QM Service Co.	PH
McMore	Earl	M	Technician 5th Cl.	462nd Amph. Truck Co.	PH
Meehan	William	F	Private 1st Cl.	3206th QM Service Co.	PH
Megathlin	Robert	H	Technician 5th Cl.	462nd Amph. Truck Co.	PH
Mercado	Trinidad		Technician 5th Cl.	462nd Amph. Truck Co.	PH
Mettler	Harry	W	Private	3206th QM Service Co.	PH
Metz	Charles Jr	E	Technician 5th Cl.	35th Signal Construction Bn	PH
Meurer	Lawrence	L	Private 1st Cl.	3206th QM Service Co.	PH
Miller	James	E	Private	3206th QM Service Co.	PH
Miller	Roy	A	Technician 4th Cl.	35th Signal Construction Co.	PH

Morgan	Alvin	G	Private 1st Cl.	3206th QM Service Co.	
Murray	Hugh	C	Private 1st Cl.	3206th QM Service Co.	PH
Naccarelli	Michael	J	Private	24th Amph. Truck Bn (462nd Amph. Truck Co.)	PH
Nagel	Curtis	A	Private 1st Cl.	3206th QM Service Co.	PH
New	Robert	T	Private	3206th QM Service Co.	PH
Newman	Aubrey	L	Private 1st Cl.	3206th QM Service Co.	PH
Newman	John	D	Technician 5th Cl.	35th Signal Construction Co.	PH
Niedermeir	Clarence			607th Graves Registration Co.	
Ogden	Ubron	M	Private	462nd Amph. Truck Co.	PH
Ostrowski	Joseph	L	Private 1st Cl.	462nd Amph. Truck Co.	PH
Ott	Lawrence	W	Private 1st Cl.	3206th QM Service Co.	PH
Overton	Delbert	E	Private	3206th QM Service Co.	PH
Owens	Johnnie	D	Private	3206th QM Service Co.	PH
Park	James	E	Private	3206th QM Service Co.	PH
Park	Clifford	F	Private	531st Engineer Shore Regt.	
Patou	Louis	S	Private 1st Cl.	625th Ordnance Ammunition Co.	PH
Payton	Marvin	L	Private	3206th QM Service Co.	PH
Peake	Cleo	B	Private 1st Cl.	3206th QM Service Co.	PH
Pearson	Luther	M	Private	3206th QM Service Co.	PH
Penalver	Joe	V	Private	3206th QM Service Co.	
Penn	Milton		Private 1st Cl.	3206th QM Service Co.	PH
Pentecost	Curtis		Private	556th QM RH Co.	
Peters	Lindsay Jr		2nd Lieutenant	3206th QM Service Co.	PH
Peters	Gerrit Jr		Technician 5th Cl.	531st Engineer Shore Regt.	PH
Picking	Charles	R	Corporal	3206th QM Service Co.	PH
Poggi	Alfred	E	Corporal	3206th QM Service Co.	PH
Poore	Winford	J	Staff Sergeant	35th Signal Construction Bn	PH
Pope	Edgar	F	Technician 4th Cl.	3206th QM Service Co.	
Pshenitzky	Charles	J	Private	3206th QM Service Co.	PH
Raines	Thomas	E	Private	3206th QM Service Co.	PH
Ray	Ulton	A	Technician 5th Cl.	462nd Amph. Truck Co.	PH
Reese	William	R	1st Sergeant	3206th QM Service Co.	PH
Reitzel	Walter	W	Private	3206th QM Service Co.	PH
Renner	Lowell	L	Private 1st Cl.	3206th QM Service Co.	PH
Rettinger	Irving		Private 1st Cl.	3206th QM Service Co.	PH
Rice	Playford	R	Private 1st Cl.	35th Signal Construction Co.	PH
Richardson	Alvin	F	Private	3206th QM Service Co.	PH
Riggs	Robert	R	Private 1st Cl.	462nd Amph. Truck Co.	PH
Riter	Edward	L	Private	35th Signal Construction Co.	PH
Roberson	James	E	Private	3206th QM Service Co.	PH
Roberson	Melvin	A	Private	3206th QM Service Co.	
Roberts	Ralph	R	Private	3206th QM Service Co.	PH
Rodriguez	Aristedes		Private 1st Cl.	3206th QM Service Co.	PH

Rohrbaugh	Tracy	V	Private 1st Cl.	625th Ordnance Ammunition Co.	PH
Roper	Rudolph	J	Private	3206th QM Service Co.	PH
Ruediger	Harry		Technician 5th Cl.	462nd Amph. Truck Co.	PH
Salemmo	Raymond	G	Private 1st Cl.	3206th QM Service Co.	PH
Sanders	Elmer	J	Private 1st Cl.	607th Graves Registration Co.	
Sandford	Harold	L	Private	3206th QM Service Co.	PH
Schleyer	Richard	C	Private	462nd Amph. Truck Co.	PH
Schmidt	Marcus	W	Private 1st Cl.	35th Signal Construction Bn	PH
Schultheis	Carl	L	Private	462nd Amph. Truck Co.	PH
Sessamen	Joseph	H	Private	462nd Amph. Truck Co.	PH
Sharff	Willard	C	Corporal	3206th QM Service Co.	PH
Sheahan	John	P	Private 1st Cl.	3206th QM Service Co.	PH
Siatkowski	Michael	J	Private 1st Cl.	462nd Amph. Truck Co.	PH
Simmons	Leland		Private 1st Cl.	531st Engineer Shore Regt.	PH
Sitche	George	R	Private	3206th QM Service Co.	PH
Slusher	Carl	W	Technical Sergeant	35th Signal Construction Bn	PH
Smerek	Steve	L	Corporal	3206th QM Service Co.	PH
Smith	Jesse	E	Private 1st Cl.	625th Ordnance Ammunition Co.	PH
Smith	Wallace	W	Private 1st Cl.	3206th QM Service Co.	PH
Snider	Donald	E	Private	462nd Amph. Truck Co.	PH
Snyder	Wallace	F	Captain	3206th QM Service Co.	
Sparks	William	F	Private 1st Cl.	3206th QM Service Co.	PH
Spurling	James	W	Private 1st Cl.	3206th QM Service Co.	PH
Steen	George	W	Private	531st Engineer Shore Regt.	PH
Stephenson	James	William	Private 1st Cl.	3206th QM Service Co.	PH
Stevens	Marshall	L	Private 1st Cl.	531st Engineer Shore Regt.	
Stillwell	Elmer	D	Technician 5th Cl.	607th Graves Registration Co.	PH
Strader	Glen	T	Private	625th Ordnance Ammunition Co.	PH
Summerall	Marvin	L	Technician 5th Cl.	462nd Amph. Truck Co.	PH
Sutphin	Claude	R	Private	35th Signal Construction Co.	PH
Sutt	Lennie	C	Private	3206th QM Service Co.	PH
Sweeney	Myles	E	Private	557th RH Co.	PH
Tate	Owen	A	Private	3206th QM Service Co.	PH
Tenuta	Louis	A	Private	3206th QM Service Co.	PH
Tesoriero	Joseph	A	Private	3206th QM Service Co.	PH
Tetreault	Rene	W	Technician 5th Cl.	35th Signal Construction Co.	PH
Thomas	Fay	E	Private 1st Cl.	3206th QM Service Co.	
Thompson	Ernest	M	Private 1st Cl.	607th Graves Registration Co.	PH

Toerber	Mearl	L	Private 1st Cl.	3206th QM Service Co.	PH
Tolie	John	N	Private 1st Cl.	3206th QM Service Co.	PH
Torres	Victor	M	Corporal	3206th QM Service Co.	PH
Tousignant	Joseph	H	Private	531st Engineer Shore Regt.	PH
Trager	Jacob		Private 1st Cl.	3206th QM Service Co.	PH
Treef	Stanley	H	Private	3206th QM Service Co.	PH
Tucker	Luther	R	Private	3206th QM Service Co.	PH
Turk	William	A	Private	3206th QM Service Co.	PH
Tuttle	Hillard		Private 1st Cl.	531st Engineer Shore Regt.	PH
Van Ess	Simon		Technician 5th Cl.	462nd Amph. Truck Co.	PH
Van Nostrand	Clarence	M	Technician 5th Cl.	462nd Amph. Truck Co.	PH
Wagner	Howard	W	Private	3206th QM Service Co.	PH+OLC
Walker	Denver		Private 1st Cl.	625th Ordnance Ammunition Co.	PH
Ward	Luther	T	Private 1st Cl.	607th Graves Registration Co.	
Watson	Gerald	A	Private	3206th QM Service Co.	PH
Webb	Grady, Jr	D	Private	531st Engineer Shore Regt.	PH
Weir	Larry	R	Private	607th Graves Registration Co.	PH
Whetstine	Everett	E	Private 1st Cl.	3206th QM Service Co.	PH
Whitelock	William	L	Private	3206th QM Service Co.	PH
Williams	Horace	S	Corporal	3206th QM Service Co.	
Wilson	Raymond	B	Private 1st Cl.	3206th QM Service Co.	PH
Wilson	Paul	W	Private 1st Cl.	3206th QM Service Co.	PH
Wilson	Kenneth	P	Technician 5th Cl.	35th Signal Construction Co.	PH
Wilson	Vernon	S.	Private 1st Cl.	3206th QM Service Co.	PH
Wintjen	Floyd	E	Private 1st Cl.	3206th QM Service Co.	PH
Wirth	Russell	L	Private	3206th QM Service Co.	PH
Wolfgram	Henry	F	Technician 5th Cl.	462nd Amph. Truck Co.	PH
Wolpert	Frederick	J	Private	3206th QM Service Co.	PH
Wooderson	Darryl	V	Private 1st Cl.	3206th QM Service Co.	PH
Wright	Myron Jr	A	Private 1st Cl.	3207th QM Service Co.	PH
Wyckoff	John	E	Private 1st Cl.	462nd Amph. Truck Co.	PH
Yadrich	Mike	J	Private 1st Cl.	3206th QM Service Co.	PH
Yates	John	W	Sergeant	3206th QM Service Co.	PH
Yates	Phillip	R	Technician 4th Cl.	35th Signal Construction Co.	PH

US Navy

Last	First	Middle	Rank	Unit	Decoration
Achey	Allen Jr	Obe	Motor Mach. Mate, 3rd Cl.	US Naval Reserve	
Anderson	Willard	Cecil	Seaman, 1st Cl.	US Naval Reserve	PH
Baugher	Ellis	Warren	Hosp. Apprentice 2nd Cl.	US Naval Reserve	PH
Behrens	John	Willy	Lieutenant	US Navy	PH
Benton	Elmer	Charles	Seaman, 1st Cl.	US Naval Reserve	
Bliss	Arthur	Harry	Seaman, 2nd Cl.	US Naval Reserve	PH

Bolling	Floyd	Howard	Seaman, 1st Cl.	US Naval Reserve	
Borgerson	Raymond		Gunners Mate 3rd Cl.	US Naval Reserve	PH
Brecheisen	Calvin	D	Technician 5th Cl.	3206th QM Service Co.	
Brickey	William	Earl	Coxswain	US Navy	PH
Bridgham	Wade	Laurence	QM, 3rd Cl.	US Naval Reserve	PH
Brock	Norris	Grant	Seaman, 1st Cl.	US Naval Reserve	
Brummitt	Clifton Jnr	Henry	Seaman, 1st Cl.	US Naval Reserve	
Callos	Vincent	Male	Coxswain		
Cantrell	William	Howard	Ensign	US Naval Reserve	PH
Carr	Frederick	Cecil	Coxswain	US Naval Reserve	
Cason	Paskel	Oliver	Seaman, 1st Cl.	US Naval Reserve	PH
Christoffel	Raymond	J	Coxswain	US Navy	PH
Cobern	William	Wheeler	Motor Mach. Mate, 3rd Cl.	US Naval Reserve	PH
Colwell	Richard	LaVerne	Seaman, 2nd Cl.	US Naval Reserve	PH
Corideo	Richard	Vincent	Seaman, 1st Cl.	US Naval Reserve	PH
Cowan	Eugene	Rice	Coxswain	US Naval Reserve	
Coyle	Michael	J	Baker 3rd Cl.	US Naval Reserve	PH
Cram	Archer	Frederick	Ensign	US Naval Reserve	PH
Croswell	Curtis	Wilton	Seaman, 1st Cl.	US Naval Reserve	PH
Cruz	Joseph Jr		Motor Mach. Mate, 3rd Cl.	US Naval Reserve	PH
Cummings	Eugene	Francis	Motor Mach. Mate, 2nd Cl.	US Naval Reserve	PH
Czerwinski	William	Joseph	Fireman, 1st Cl.	US Naval Reserve	PH
Danley	Harry	I		US Naval Reserve	
Dawson	Glenn	Hunter	Hosp. Apprentice 2nd Cl.	US Navy	
DeBias	Edward	George	Coxswain	US Naval Reserve	
DeGouff	Theodore	Denis	Seaman, 1st Cl.	US Naval Reserve	PH
Denton	Harold	Clifford	Soundman, 3rd Cl.	US Naval Reserve	
Dobson	Edwin	James	Seaman, 1st Cl.	US Navy	PH
Drake	Robert	George	Coxswain	US Naval Reserve	PH
Duffy	Ralph	O'Connell	Gunners Mate 2nd Cl.	US Naval Reserve	PH
Edson	Richard	Wyman	Seaman, 1st Cl.	US Naval Reserve	
Ellis	John	J	Seaman, 1st Cl.	US Naval Reserve	PH
Fisher	E.	C.	Stewards Mate 2nd Cl.	US Naval Reserve	PH
Ford	Hobart Jr		Gunners Mate 2nd Cl.	US Navy	PH
Gaboys	Edward	Arthur	Seaman, 1st Cl.	US Naval Reserve	PH
Gallagher	John	J	Ensign	US Naval Reserve	
Goldstein	Samuel		Hosp. Apprentice 2nd Cl.	US Naval Reserve	PH
Gunn	Murray	S	Pharm. Mate 1st Cl.	US Naval Reserve	PH
Hall	William	Cornelius	Pharm. Mate 3rd Cl.	US Naval Reserve	PH
Harrell	Charles		Hosp. Apprentice 2nd Cl.	US Naval Reserve	PH
Hartman	Robert	Joseph	Radioman, 3rd Cl.	US Naval Reserve	PH
Hauber	Bernard	Anthony	Electricians Mate 2nd Cl.	US Naval Reserve	
Hayth	Eugene		Shipfitter, 2nd Cl.	US Naval Reserve	
Hill	John	H	Lieutenant, JG	US Naval Reserve	
Hopkins	Lawrence	Elmer	Seaman, 2nd Cl.	US Naval Reserve	PH

Hurley	James	W	Hosp. Apprentice 2nd Cl.	US Naval Reserve	
Jackman	Walter Jr	P	Ensign	US Naval Reserve	
Jacques	Edmond	Leopold	Seaman, 2nd Cl.	US Naval Reserve	PH
Jansen	Melvin	John	Seaman, 1st Cl.	US Naval Reserve	PH
Jencovic	Albert	Joseph	Seaman, 2nd Cl.	US Naval Reserve	PH
Johnson	Albert Jr	W	Radioman, 3rd Cl.	US Naval Reserve	PH
Kartz	Henry		Boatswains Mate, 2nd Cl.	US Naval Reserve	SS, PH
Kaska	Albert	Paul	Seaman, 1st Cl.	US Navy	PH
Kelley	Ford	Henry	Seaman, 2nd Cl.	US Naval Reserve	
Kerby	Reuben	Grady	Seaman, 2nd Cl.	US Naval Reserve	PH
Kessinger	Mark	Frederick	Seaman, 2nd Cl.	US Naval Reserve	
Kirby	Grady	Eldridge	Seaman, 2nd Cl.	US Naval Reserve	PH
Kirkwood	Ralph	August	Fireman, 2nd Cl.	US Naval Reserve	PH
Krizanosky	Alexander		Fireman, 2nd Cl.	US Naval Reserve	
Kuhns	Harold	Duncan	Seaman, 2nd Cl.	US Naval Reserve	
Lacey	Burvil	Elver	Seaman, 1st Cl.	US Naval Reserve	
Land	Charles	Garner	Seaman, 2nd Cl.	US Naval Reserve	
Leeman	Hollace	Hebron	Hosp. Apprentice 2nd Cl.	US Naval Reserve	PH
Levine	Harry		Hosp. Apprentice 1st Cl.	US Naval Reserve	
Levy	Lester	Harold	Lieutenant	US Naval Reserve	
Locklear	Melvin	Levertt	Chief Commissary Steward	US Navy	
Manning	Tiffany	Vincent	Lieutenant, JG	US Naval Reserve	PH
Marcus	Emery Jr	Eugene	Ships Cook 3rd Cl.	US Naval Reserve	PH
McCuen	Frank	Alfred	Motor Mach. Mate, 1st Cl.	US Naval Reserve	
McLean	Robert	William	Motor Mach. Mate, 2nd Cl.		
Merrill	William	Joseph	Hosp. Apprentice 2nd Cl.	US Naval Reserve	PH
Miller	Ralph	Rudisill	Coxswain	US Navy	
Montgomery	Doyle	David	Yeoman, 1st Cl.	US Naval Reserve	
Neal	Kermit	Harold	Hosp. Apprentice 2nd Cl.	US Naval Reserve	PH
Nelson	Lee	Otis	Ensign	US Naval Reserve	PH
Noble	Elisha	George	Stewards Mate 1st Cl.	US Naval Reserve	PH
Parker	Cornelius	Judson	Motor Mach. Mate, 2nd Cl.	US Naval Reserve	
Pear	William		Electricians Mate 3rd Cl.	US Naval Reserve	
Petcavage	William	Joseph	Seaman, 1st Cl.	US Naval Reserve	PH
Peters	James	Donald	Coxswain	US Naval Reserve	
Peterson	Robert	Donald	Motor Mach. Mate, 3rd Cl.	US Naval Reserve	PH
Phillips	Kenneth		Motor Mach. Mate, 3rd Cl.	US Naval Reserve	PH
Pogue	Richard		Fireman, 2nd Cl.	US Naval Reserve	PH
Poloncarz	John	Edward	Seaman, 1st Cl.	US Naval Reserve	PH
Rugani	Daniel	Louis	Hosp. Apprentice 2nd Cl.	US Naval Reserve	PH
Samuelson	Gail	Earl	Hosp. Apprentice 2nd Cl.	US Naval Reserve	PH

Schimanske	Daniel	Richard	Gunners Mate 3rd Cl.		
Scott	James	Oliver		US Naval Reserve	PH
Shea	John	Maurice	QM, 3rd Cl.	US Naval Reserve	PH
Shengarn	George		Motor Mach. Mate, 3rd Cl.	US Naval Reserve	PH
Sheppard	Thanuel	Vasco	Gunners Mate 3rd Cl.	US Naval Reserve	PH
Showers	Lyle	Foster	Pharm. Mate 3rd Cl.	US Naval Reserve	
Sochacki	Edward	Anthony	Pharm. Mate 2nd Cl.	US Naval Reserve	
Solomon	William		Hosp. Apprentice 1st Cl.	US Naval Reserve	
Spangler	Walter	Arnold	Coxswain	US Naval Reserve	PH
Starr	Joseph Jr	Louis	Motor Mach. Mate, 2nd Cl.	US Navy	PH
Stemats	Steve	Joseph	Radioman, 3rd Cl.	US Naval Reserve	
Stoklosa	Edward	Henry	Hosp. Apprentice 2nd Cl.	US Naval Reserve	PH
Taylor	George	Wesley	Seaman, 2nd Cl.	US Naval Reserve	PH
Townsend	Willie	Winsfield	Stewards Mate 2nd Cl.	US Naval Reserve	PH
Unger	Alvin	Charles	Storekeeper, 3rd Cl.	US Navy	
Vendeland	Albert	Jerome	Seaman, 1st Cl.	US Naval Reserve	
Walls	James	Washington	Seaman, 2nd Cl.	US Naval Reserve	PH
Walters	Robert	Gerald	Ships Cook 3rd Cl.	US Naval Reserve	PH
Watson	Raleigh	Frank	Seaman, 2nd Cl.	US Naval Reserve	PH
Waugh	James	Norton	Seaman, 1st Cl.	US Naval Reserve	
White	Earnest	Turner	Electricians Mate 3rd Cl.	US Naval Reserve	PH
Witten	Lloyd	L	Chief Pharm. Mate	US Navy	PH
Carroll	Francis	A	Motor Mach.	US Naval Reserve	PH

Technical Specifications for main vessels involved in Exercise Tiger

US Navy Vessels

LST-58

LST-1 Class Tank Landing Ship:
Laid down: 31 October 1943, at Dravo Corp., Pittsburgh, PA.;
Launched: 11 December 1943;
Commissioned: USS LST-58, 22 January 1944.
During World War II, LST-58 was assigned to the European theatre and participated in the Invasion of Normandy, June 1944.
Decommissioned: 7 November 1945;
Struck from the Naval Register: 28 November 1945;
Final Disposition, sold for scrapping: 30 November 1947, to Northern Metals Co., Philadelphia, PA.
Honours: one battle star for World War II service.
Commander at the time of Exercise Tiger (if known): Lieutenant John Wachter.

Specifications:
Displacement: 1,780 t.(lt), 3,880 t.(fl);
Length: 328 feet; Beam: 50 feet;
Draft unloaded: bow 2 feet 4 inches stern 7 feet 6 inches, loaded bow 8 feet 2 inches stern 14 feet 1 inch;
Speed: 12k.; Complement: 8-10 Officers, 100-115 Enlisted;
Troop Capacity: approx. 140 officers and enlisted;
Boats: 2-6 LCVP;
Armament: one single 3 inches/50 gun mount, five 40 mm gun mounts, six 20 mm gun mounts, two .50-cal machine guns, four .30-cal machine guns;
Propulsion: two General Motors 12-567 diesel engines, two shafts, twin rudders.

LST-289

LST-1 Class Tank Landing Ship:

Laid down: 14 September 1943, at the American Bridge Co., Ambridge, MA;

Launched: 21 November 1943;

Commissioned: USS LST-289, 31 December 1943,

During World War II USS LST-289 was assigned to the Europe-Africa-Middle East Theatre; Severely damaged by a German E-Boat torpedo attack off Slapton Sands, England, 28 April 1944, during Operation Tiger, the rehearsal for the Normandy invasion;

Decommissioned and transferred to the United Kingdom: 30 November 1944

Royal Navy History: Commissioned into the Royal Navy as HM LST-289: 30 November 1944

De-equipped and mud-berthed at Sandacre Bay: 30 July 1946

Paid off and returned to US Navy custody: 12 October 1946

Struck from the Naval Register: 15 October 1946

Final Disposition: sold, 30 January 1947 to the Netherlands as MV Fendracht

Commander at the time of Exercise Tiger (if known): Lieutenant Harry Mettler

Specifications: (as reported by Office of Naval Intelligence-1945):

Displacement: 1,625 t.(lt), 4,080 t.(fl) (sea-going draft w/1675 ton load);

Length: 328 feet o.a.; Beam: 50 feet;

Draft: (light)—2 feet 4 inches fwd, 7 feet 6 inches aft, (sea-going) 8 feet 3 inches fwd, 14 feet 1 inch aft, (landing) 3 feet 11 inch fwd, 9 feet 10 inches aft (landing w/500 ton load);

Speed: 12 kts. (maximum);

Endurance: 24,000 miles @ 9kts. while displacing 3,960 tons;

Complement: 7 officers, 104 enlisted

Troop Accommodations: 16 officers, 147 enlisted;

Boats: two LCVP;

Cargo Capacity varied with mission—payloads between 1,600 and 1,900 tons)

Typical loads: One Landing Craft Tank (LCT), tanks, wheeled and tracked vehicles, artillery, construction equipment and military supplies. A ramp or elevator forward allowed vehicles access to tank deck from main deck. Additional capacity included sectional pontoons carried on each side of vessel amidships, to either build Rhino Barges or use as causeways. Married to the bow ramp, the causeways would enable payloads to be delivered ashore from deeper water or where a beachhead would not allow the vessel to be grounded forward after ballasting;

Armament: varied with availability when each vessel was outfitted. Retro-fitting was accomplished throughout World War II. The ultimate armament design for United States vessels was: two Twin 40 mm, gun mounts w/Mk.51 directors, four Single 40 mm gun mounts, and twelve single 20 mm gun mounts.

LST-496

LST-1 Class Tank Landing Ship:

Laid down: 24 August 1943, at Missouri Valley Bridge and Iron Co., Evansville, IN.;

Launched: 22 October 1943;

Commissioned USS LST-496: 27 December 1943.

During World War II, LST-496 was assigned to the European theatre and participated in the invasion of Normandy, June 1944. She was sunk by enemy mines off Omaha Beach, Normandy, on 11 June 1944.

Struck from the Naval Register: 22 August 1944.

LST-496 earned one battle star for World War II service.

Specifications:

Displacement: 1,780 t. (lt), 3,640 t. (fl);

Length: 328 feet; Beam: 50 feet;

Draft: unloaded, bow 2 feet 4 inches stern 7 feet 6 inches, loaded bow 8 feet 2 inches stern 14 feet 1 inch;

Speed: 12k.;

Complement: 8-10 Officers, 100-115 Enlisted;

Troop Capacity: approx. 140 officers and enlisted;

Boats, 2-6 LCVP;

Armament: one single 3 inches/50 gun mount, five 40 mm gun mounts, six 20 mm gun mounts, two .50-cal machine guns, four .30-cal machine guns;

Propulsion: two General Motors 12-567 diesel engines, two shafts, twin rudders.

Commander at the time of Exercise Tiger (if known): Lieutenant Stanley Koch

LST-499

LST-1 Class Tank Landing Ship:

Laid down: 3 September 1943, at Missouri Valley Bridge and Iron Co., Evansville, IN.

Launched: 5 November 1943

Commissioned: USS LST-499, 10 January 1944

During World War II USS LST-499 was assigned to the Europe-Africa-Middle East Theatre and participated in the Invasion of Normandy, June 1944

Sunk as a result of enemy action: 8 June 1944

Struck from the Naval Register: 22 August 1944

USS LST-499 earned one battle star for World War II service

Specifications (as reported by Office of Naval Intelligence–1945):

Displacement: 1,625 t. (lt), 4,080 t. (fl) (sea-going draft w/1,675 ton load);

Length: 328 feet o.a.; Beam 50 feet;

Draft: (light)—2 feet 4 inches fwd, 7 feet 6 inches aft, (sea-going) 8 feet 3 inches fwd, 14 feet 1 inch aft, (landing) 3 feet 11 inches fwd, 9 feet 10 inches aft (landing w/500 ton load);

Speed: 12 kts. (maximum);

Endurance: 24,000 miles @ 9kts. while displacing 3,960 tons;

Complement seven officers, one hundred and four enlisted;

Troop Accommodations: sixteen officers, one hundred and forty seven enlisted;

Boats: two LCVP;

Cargo Capacity: (varied with mission—payloads between 1,600 and 1,900 tons)

Typical loads: One Landing Craft Tank (LCT), tanks, wheeled and tracked vehicles, artillery, construction equipment and military supplies. A ramp or elevator forward allowed vehicles access to tank deck from main deck. Additional capacity included sectional pontoons carried on each side of vessel amidships, to either build Rhino Barges or use as causeways. Married to the bow ramp, the causeways would enable payloads to be delivered ashore from deeper water or where a beachhead would not allow the vessel to be grounded forward after ballasting;

Armament: varied with availability when each vessel was outfitted. Retro-fitting was accomplished throughout World War II. The ultimate armament design for United States vessels was two Twin 40 mm gun mounts w/Mk.51 directors, four—Single 40 gun mounts and twelve single 20 mm gun mounts; Propulsion: two General Motors 12-567, 900 hp diesel engines, two shafts, twin rudders.

LST-507

LST-1 Class Tank Landing Ship:

Laid down: 8 September 1943, at Jeffersonville Boat and Machine Co., Jeffersonville, IN.

Launched, 16 November 1943;

Commissioned: USS LST-507, 10 January 1944;

During World War II USS LST-507 was assigned to the Europe-Africa-Middle East Theatre;

Sunk by a German E-Boat torpedo attack off Slapton Sands, England, 28 April 1944, during Operation Tiger, the rehearsal for the Normandy invasion;

Struck from the Naval Register: 9 June 1944;

Commander at the time of Exercise Tiger (if known): Lieutenant James S. Swarts

Specifications (as reported by Office of Naval Intelligence-1945):

Displacement: 1,625 t. (lt), 4,080 t. (fl) (sea-going draft w/1,675 ton load);

Length: 328 feet o.a.; Beam 50 feet;

Draft (light)—2 feet 4 inches fwd, 7 feet 6 inches aft, (sea-going) 8 feet 3 inches fwd, 14 feet 1 inch aft, (landing) 3 feet 11 inches fwd, 9 feet 10 inches aft (landing w/500 ton load);

Speed: 12 kts. (maximum);

Endurance: 24,000 miles @ 9kts. while displacing 3,960 tons;

Complement: nine officers, one hundred and twenty enlisted;

Troop Accommodations: fourteen officers, one hundred and thirty one enlisted;

Boats: six LCVP;

Cargo Capacity: (varied with mission—payloads between 1600 and 1900 tons);

Typical loads: One Landing Craft Tank (LCT), tanks, wheeled and tracked vehicles, artillery, construction equipment and military supplies. A ramp or elevator forward allowed vehicles access to tank deck from main deck. Additional capacity included sectional pontoons carried on each side of vessel amidships, to either build Rhino Barges or use as causeways. Married to the bow ramp, the causeways would enable payloads to be delivered ashore from deeper water or where a beachhead would not allow the vessel to be grounded forward after ballasting;

Armament: varied with availability when each vessel was outfitted. Retro-fitting was accomplished throughout World War II; The ultimate armament design for United States vessels was: two Twin 40 mm gun mounts w/Mk.51 directors, four single 40 mm gun mounts and twelve single 20 mm gun mounts.

LST-511

LST-1 Class Tank Landing Ship:

Laid down: 22 July 1943, at Chicago Bridge and Iron Co., Seneca, IL.

Launched: 30 November 1943;

Commissioned: USS LST-511, 3 January 1944;

During World War II USS LST-511 was assigned to the European Theatre and participated in the invasion of Normandy, 6 June, 1944;

Decommissioned: 19 December 1945

Struck from the Naval Register: 8 January, 1946

Commander at the time of Exercise Tiger (if known): Lieutenant John Yacevich

Commercial Service:

Sold in 1947 to the St Charles Transportation Co., Ltd. of Quebec, Province of Quebec, Canada and named MV *Guy Bartholomew*;

Sold in 1948 to Corporation Maritime Rive-Nord, Ltd. of Quebec;

Sold in 1969 to Agence Maritime, Inc. of Quebec and renamed MV *Fort Kent*;

Sold in 1979 to Logisec Navigation, Inc. of Quebec;

Final Disposition: fate unknown

USS LST-511 earned one battle star for World War II service

Specifications (as reported by Office of Naval Intelligence–1945):

Displacement: 1,625 t. (lt), 4,080 t. (fl) (sea-going draft w/1,675 ton load);

Length: 328 feet o.a.; Beam: 50 feet;

Draft: (light)—2 feet 4 inches fwd, 7 feet 6 inches aft, (sea-going) 8 feet 3 inches fwd, 14 feet 1 inch aft, (landing) 3 feet 11 inches fwd, 9 feet 10 inches aft (landing w/500 ton load);

Speed: 12 kts. (maximum);

Endurance: 24,000 miles @ 9kts. while displacing 3,960 tons;

Complement: nine officers, one hundred and twenty enlisted;

Troop Accommodations: fourteen officers, one hundred and thirty one enlisted;

Boats: four LCVP;

Cargo Capacity (varied with mission—payloads between 1,600 and 1,900 tons);

Typical loads: One Landing Craft Tank (LCT), tanks, wheeled and tracked vehicles, artillery, construction equipment and military supplies. A ramp or elevator forward allowed vehicles access to tank deck from main deck. Additional capacity included sectional pontoons carried on each side of vessel amidships, to either build Rhino Barges or use as causeways. Married to the bow ramp, the causeways would enable payloads to be delivered ashore from deeper water or where a beachhead would not allow the vessel to be grounded forward after ballasting;

Armament: varied with availability when each vessel was outfitted. Retro-fitting was accomplished throughout World War II; The ultimate armament design for United States vessels was: two twin 40 mm gun mounts w/Mk.51 directors; four single 40 mm gun mounts and twelve single 20 mm gun mounts. Lend Lease built vessels were to be outfitted with armament after convoying across Atlantic and included one Twelve-Pounder anti-aircraft multi-barrel mount, six 20 mm mounts and four Fast Aerial Mine (FAM) mounts.

Propulsion: two General Motors 12-567, 900 hp diesel engines, two shafts, twin rudders.

LST-*515*

LST-1 Class Tank Landing Ship:

Laid down: 3 September 1943, at Chicago Bridge and Iron Co., Seneca, IL.

Launched: 31 December 1943;

Commissioned USS LST-*515*: 28 January 1944

During World War II, LST-*515* was assigned to the Europe-Africa-Middle East Theatre and participated in the invasion of Normandy, 6 to 25 June, 1944;

Following World War II USS LST-*515* performed occupation duty in the Far East until November 1952;

Named USS *Caddo Parish* (LST-*515*): 1 July, 1955

Decommissioned: 20 October 1955

Recommissioned: 2 August 1963

USS *Caddo Parish* (LST-*515*) participated in several Vietnam War campaigns from 1965 through to 1969

Transferred to the Philippine Navy: 26 November 1969, renamed RPS *Bataan* (LT-85)

Decommissioned: date unknown

Struck from the Naval Register: date unknown

Final Disposition: fate unknown

Honours: earned one battle star for World War II service and as USS *Caddo Parish* (LST-*515*) received the Navy Unit Commendation, the Navy Meritorious Unit Commendation, and nine campaign stars for Vietnam War service

Commander at the time of Exercise Tiger (if known): Lieutenant John Doyle

Specifications (as reported by Office of Naval Intelligence–1945):

Displacement: 1,625 t. (lt), 4,080 t. (fl) (sea-going draft w/1,675 ton load);

Length: 328 feet o.a.; Beam: 50 feet;

Draft: (light)—2 feet 4 inches fwd, 7 feet 6 inches aft, (sea-going) 8 feet 3 inches fwd, 14 feet 1 inch aft, (landing) 3 feet 11 inches fwd, 9 feet 10 inches aft (landing w/500 ton load);

Speed: 12 kts. (maximum);

Endurance: 24,000 miles @ 9kts. while displacing 3,960 tons;

Complement: seven officers, one hundred and four enlisted;

Troop Accommodations: sixteen officers, one hundred and forty seven enlisted;

Boats: two LCVP;

Cargo Capacity (varied with mission—payloads between 1,600 and 1,900 tons);

Typical loads: One Landing Craft Tank (LCT), tanks, wheeled and tracked vehicles, artillery, construction equipment and military supplies. A ramp or elevator forward allowed vehicles access to tank deck from main deck. Additional capacity included sectional pontoons carried on each side of vessel amidships, to either build Rhino Barges or use as causeways. Married to the bow ramp, the causeways would enable payloads to be delivered ashore from deeper water or where a beachhead would not allow the vessel to be grounded forward after ballasting;

Armament: varied with availability when each vessel was outfitted. Retro-fitting was accomplished throughout World War II. The ultimate armament design for United States vessels was two twin 40 mm gun mounts w/Mk.51 directors, four single

40 mm gun mounts and twelve single 20 mm gun mounts;

Propulsion: two General Motors 12-567, 900 hp diesel engines, two shafts, twin rudders.

LST-531

LST-1 Class Tank Landing Ship:

Laid down: 22 September 1943, at Missouri Valley Bridge and Iron Co., Evansville, IN.

Launched: 24 November 1943;

Commissioned USS LST-531: 17 January 1944;

During World War II USS LST-531 was assigned to the European-Africa-Middle East Theatre;

Sunk by a German E-Boat torpedo attack off Slapton Sands, England, 28 April 1944, during Operation Tiger, the rehearsal for the Normandy invasion;

Struck from the Naval Register: 9 June 1944

Commander at the time of Exercise Tiger (if known): Lieutenant John W. Behrens

Specifications (as reported by Office of Naval Intelligence-1945):

Displacement: 1,625 t. (lt), 4,080 t. (fl) (sea-going draft w/1675 ton load);

Length: 328 feet o.a.; Beam: 50 feet;

Draft: (light)—2 feet 4 inches fwd, 7 feet 6 inches aft, (sea-going) 8 feet 3 inches fwd, 14 feet 1 inch aft, (landing) 3 feet 11 inches fwd, 9 feet 10 inches aft (landing w/500 ton load);

Speed: 12 kts. (maximum);

Endurance: 24,000 miles @ 9kts. while displacing 3,960 tons;

Complement: nine officers, one hundred and twenty enlisted;

Troop Accommodations: fourteen officers, one hundred and thirty one enlisted;

Boats: six LCVP;

Cargo Capacity (varied with mission—payloads between 1600 and 1900 tons)

Typical loads: One Landing Craft Tank (LCT), tanks, wheeled and tracked vehicles, artillery, construction equipment and military supplies. A ramp or elevator forward allowed vehicles access to tank deck from main deck. Additional capacity included sectional pontoons carried on each side of vessel amidships, to either build Rhino Barges or use as causeways. Married to the bow ramp, the causeways would enable payloads to be delivered ashore from deeper water or where a beachhead would not allow the vessel to be grounded forward after ballasting;

Armament: varied with availability when each vessel was outfitted. Retro-fitting was accomplished throughout World War II. The ultimate armament design for United States vessels was: two twin 40 mm gun mounts w/Mk.51 directors, four single 40 mm gun mounts and twelve single 20 mm gun mounts.

USS *Bayfield*

Bayfield-class attack transport:

Laid down: 14 November 1942, at Western Pipe and Steel, San Francisco, California as coast-guard vessel.

Launched: 15 February 1943 with coast guard crew;

Commissioned as USS *Sea Bass*: 20 November 1943;

Converted to Naval Auxiliary Vessel: 30 November 1943 and renamed USS
  Bayfield;

During World War II USS *Bayfield* was assigned to the European, Mediterranean
  and Pacific Theatres, participating in Normandy Landings, Invasion of Southern
  France, Invasions of Iwo Jima and Okinawa;

Post World War II, USS *Bayfield* took part in atomic testing at Bikini Atoll, then
  went back into the Pacific during Korean War;

In 1962, USS *Bayfield* provided support for the quarantine of Cuba during the
  missile crisis;

During Vietnam War, USS *Bayfield* acted as floating barracks, as well as troop
  transport ship;

Decommissioned: 28 June 1968;

Struck from Naval Register: 1 October 1968

Honours: Four battle starts for service during World War II, four for Korean War
  and two for Vietnam War.

Commander at the time of Exercise Tiger (if known): Captain Lyndon Spencer
  (USCG)

Specifications:

Displacement: 8,100 t. (lt), 16,100 t. (fl)

Length: 492 feet;

Beam: 69 feet 6 inches;

Draft: 26 feet 6 inches;

Speed: 18 kts.;

Complement: Crew—51 officers, 524 enlisted; Flag—43 officers, 108 enlisted;
  Troops—80 officers, 1,146 enlisted

Boats: 12 x LCVP, 4 x LCM, 3 x LCP(L);

Capacity: 200,000 cubic feet;

Armament: 2 x singe 5 inch/38 cal. dual purpose gun mounts, one fore and one aft;
  2 x twin 40 mm AA gun mounts forward, port and starboard, 2 x single 40 mm
  AA gun mounts; 18 x single 20 mm AA gun mounts.

USS *Augusta*

Northampton-class heavy cruiser:

Laid down: 2 July 1928, at Newport News Shipbuilding and Dry Dock Co, Virginia.

Launched: 1 February 1930;

Commissioned: 30 January 1931;

During World War II USS *Augusta* was assigned to the European, North African and
  Atlantic Theatres, participating in Operation Torch, the Normandy Landings, and
  Operation Dragoon;

Operated as Presidential Flagship;

Decommissioned: 16 July 1946;

Struck from Naval Register: 1 March 1959

Honours: Three Battle Stars for service in World War II

Commander at the time of Exercise Tiger (if known): Commander J. L. Phares

Specifications:

Displacement: 9,200 t.

Length: 570 feet (waterline); 600 feet 3 inches (overall);

Beam: 66 feet 1 inch;

Draft: 16 feet 6 inches (mean); 23 feet (max);

Speed: 32.7 kts.;

Complement: 105 Officers, 995 Enlisted

Boats: 12 x LCVP, 4 x LCM, 3 x LCP(L);

Armament: 9 x 8 in/55 cal guns (3x3), 8 x 5 in/25 cal AA guns, 32 x 40 mm AA guns, 27 x 20 mm AA cannons;

Aircraft Carried: 4 x SOC Seagull scout-observation seaplanes.

Royal Navy Ships

HMS *Azalea*

Flower-class corvette

Laid down: 15 November 1939 by Cook, Welton & Gemmel of Beverley, Yorkshire

Launched: 8 July 1940;

Commissioned: 27 January 1941

During World War II, served in the European theatre

After World War II, *Azalea* was sold on 5 April 1946

Renamed: MV *Norte*

Sank on 19 January 1955

Commander at the time of Exercise Tiger (if known): Lieutenant-Commander George C. Geddes

HMS *Saladin*

S-Class destroyer

Laid down: 10 September 1917 by Alexander Stephen and Sons, Linthouse, Govan;

Launched: 17 February 1919;

Completed: 11 April 1919;

Sold for breaking up: 29 June 1947.

Commander at the time of Exercise Tiger (if known): Lieutenant-Commander Philip Geoffrey Colet King

HMS *Scimitar*

S-Class destroyer

Laid down: 30 May 1917 by John Brown and Company, Clydebank;

Launched: 27 February 1918;

Commissioned: 29 April 1918;

On 8 July 1940, HMS *Scimitar*, together with HMS *Vanquisher* picked up 43 survivors from the British merchant ship *Humber Arm* that had been torpedoed and sunk by a German U-boat 60 nautical miles south of Fastnet.

29 June 1941—A German U-boat was sunk south of Iceland by depth charges from several destroyers and corvettes, including HMS *Scimitar*.

Sold for breaking up: 29 June 1947.

Commander at the time of Exercise Tiger (if known): Lieutenant Philip Archer Shee

HMS *Obedient*

O-Class destroyer
Laid down: 22 May 1940 by William Denny & Brothers, Dumbarton;
Launched: 30 April 1942
Engaged German heavy cruiser *Admiral Hipper* on 31 December 1942 in Battle of
the Barents Sea;
Broken up 19 October1962.
Commander at the time of Exercise Tiger (if known): Lieutenant-Commander
Harold Unwin DSC

E-boats

Boats involved in Exercise Tiger: S-*100*, S-*130*, S-*136*, S-*138*, S-*140*, S-*142*, S-*143*,
S-*145*, and S-*150*
The S-Boot class 1939/1940 was the largest class of fast attack boats built
in Germany during the war. Built between 1940 and 1945, those boats were
modified based on the experience of war action, especially the light flak
armament was tripled in the later boats. Powered by the 20 cyl Daimler Benz
Diesel, they were able to archive speed above 40 kn.
From S-*100* on, the boats were equipped with an armoured control platform to
protect the crew from attacks of British MGB and MTB.
Most of the more than 100 boats built were lost during the war, either through
mine hits, battles with British ships or air attacks. The surviving boats were given
to various countries after the war, the Soviet Union used several of them until the
1950s, other boats were given to Norway or Denmark. Some few boats were later
returned to the German Bundesmarine where they served as experimental ships.
The boats from S-100 on were from the outset constructed with Kalotte. The type
S-*100* was equipped with the newly developed Diesel MB 2,500 with 2,500 hp.
Shipyards: Lürssen/Travemünde, Germany
Length: 32.76 m
Beam: 5.06 m Draught: 1.47 m
Displacement: 100 t
Propulsion S-*100* to S-*136*: 3 x Daimler-Benz MB 501 Diesel-Engines; 3,960 hp
Propulsion S-*139* to S-*150*: 3 x Daimler- Benz MB 501 A
Speed: 38,5 kn
Range: 800nm at 30 kn
Complement: 21—30
Armament: 2 x Torpedo tubes 53.3 cm (4 torpedoes); astern: 1 x 37 mm Flak 42
cannon; amidships: 1 x twin 20 mm cannon; bow: 1 x 20 mm cannon

Notes on Sources

Almost all of the images and documents used in writing this book are those that have been provided to the Exercise Tiger Trust and, all reasonable efforts have been made to contact the copyright holders for permission, where applicable. The author apologises for any errors and omissions.

Chapter One: Over Here

Sources:
http://news.bbc.co.uk/onthisday/hi/dates/stories/december/1/newsid_3535000/
    3535949.stm;
Morgan, *Overture to Overlord* (Garden City: Doubleday & Company, Inc, 1950);
Alfred Chandler, ed., *The Papers of Dwight David Eisenhower*; *The War Years*, Vol
    III (Baltimore: Johns Hopkins University Press, 1970), *King, A Naval Record*;
Harrison, *Cross-Channel Attack*, and William Leahy, *I Was There*, (New York:
    McGraw-Hill, 1950);
Letters of Lieutenant (JG) John Hill, held by Exercise Tiger Trust;
Narrative of Patsy Giacchi—www.mikekemble.com;
First-hand account of Eugene Eckstam;
First-hand account of John Maltese, CCSU Digital Collections;
First-hand account of John Spooner;
A Short Guide to Great Britain—War and Navy Departments, Washington D.C.

Chapter Two: We'll Meet Again

Sources:
Nigel Lewis, *Channel Firing—The Tragedy of Exercise Tiger* (Penguin Books, 1990);
Robin Rose-Price and Jean Parnell, *The Land We Left Behind* (Orchard
    Publications, 2004).

Chapter Three: You'll Never Know

Sources:
The Woolacombe Memorial Press Release: Brief History, held by Exercise Tiger Trust;

US Army Centre of Military History: WWII documents, VII Exercises.

Nigel Lewis, *Channel Firing—The Tragedy of Exercise Tiger* (Penguin Books, 1990);

Chapter Four: Counting the Days

Sources:

Collins, J. Lawton—*Lightning Joe, An Autobiography*, New Orleans, Louisiana State University Press, 1979;

U.S.N.A.—Trident Scholar project report; no. 221 (1994)—The U.S. Navy in Operation Overlord under the Command of Rear Admiral Alan G. Kirk by Midshipman First Class Troy A. Shoulders, Class of 1994 U.S. Naval Academy, Annapolis, Maryland.

Chapter Five: Now is the Hour

Sources:

U.S.N.A.—Trident Scholar project report; no. 221 (1994)—The U.S. Navy in Operation Overlord under the Command of Rear Admiral Alan G. Kirk by Midshipman First Class Troy A. Shoulders, Class of 1994 U.S. Naval Academy, Annapolis, Maryland;

Nigel Lewis, *Channel Firing—The Tragedy of Exercise Tiger* (Penguin Books, 1990);

Edwin P. Hoyt, *The Invasion Before Normandy—The Secret Battle of Slapton Sands* (Robert Hale Limited, 1985);

Richard T. Bass, *Exercise Tiger—The D-Day practice landing tragedies uncovered* (Menin House, 2012);

US Army Centre of Military History: WWII documents, VII Exercises;

Lieut. J. F. Murdock Debrief Transcription (document held by Exercise Tiger Trust);

First-hand account of Angelo Crapanzano;

Narrative of Patsy Giacchi—www.mikekemble.com;

First-hand account of John Maltese, CCSU Digital Collections;

First-hand account of Eugene Eckstam;

American Heritage Lives: Devon Memories;

Clifford L. Graves, Front Line Surgeons—A History of the Third Auxiliary Surgical Group (document held by Exercise Tiger Trust);

German E-boat logs (documents held by Exercise Tiger Trust);

German Comments on Operation, 28th April 1944—Scheveningen (document held by Exercise Tiger Trust);

Statement by Second Coxswain John Cullen—HMRML 532 (document held by Exercise Tiger Trust);

Article written by Ed Panter, LST-289 & 507, Published in LST Scuttlebutt, 2002;

Statement written by Steve Sadlon for *The Sun/Sun Herald*, 24th April 2006;

Account of RAFVR Pilot, Peter Nevill (document held by Exercise Tiger Trust);

Letters from John A. Brown to Marion Irving (held by Exercise Tiger Trust— courtesy of Art and Bev Hughes);

Letter from Ensign Raymond Gosselin to Mrs Hill (held by Exercise Tiger Trust— courtesy of Art and Bev Hughes).

Chapter Six: When Johnny Comes Marching Home

Sources:

Lieut. J. F. Murdock Debrief Transcription (document held by Exercise Tiger Trust);

First-hand account of Angelo Crapanzano;

Narrative of Patsy Giacchi—www.mikekemble.com;

First-hand account of John Maltese, CCSU Digital Collections;

First-hand account of Eugene Eckstam;

American Heritage Lives: Devon Memories;

Article written by Ed Panter, LST-289 & 507, Published in LST Scuttlebutt, 2002;

Statement written by Steve Sadlon for The Sun/Sun Herald, 24th April 2006;

Nigel Lewis, *Channel Firing–The Tragedy of Exercise Tiger* (Penguin Books, 1990);

Edwin P. Hoyt, *The Invasion Before Normandy–The Secret Battle of Slapton Sands* (Robert Hale Limited, 1985);

Richard T. Bass, *Exercise Tiger–The D-Day practice landing tragedies uncovered* (Menin House, 2012);

Letters from John A. Brown to Marion Irving (held by Exercise Tiger Trust—courtesy of Art and Bev Hughes);

Letter from Ensign Raymond Gosselin to Mrs Hill (held by Exercise Tiger Trust—courtesy of Art and Bev Hughes);

Statement by Second Coxswain John Cullen—HMRML 532 (document held by Exercise Tiger Trust);

First-hand account of John Spooner.

Chapter Seven: It Could Happen to You

Sources:

Statement by Second Coxswain John Cullen—HMRML 532 (document held by Exercise Tiger Trust);

Letters from John A. Brown to Marion Irving (held by Exercise Tiger Trust—courtesy of Art and Bev Hughes);

Ken Small & Mark Rogerson, *The Forgotten Dead: 60th Anniversary Edition: Why 946 American Servicemen Died Off the Coast of Devon in 1944–and the Man Who Discovered Their True Story* (Bloomsbury Publishing Plc, 2004);

Correspondence between Eugene Eckstam and Dale Rodman, held by Exercise Tiger Trust;

Edwin P. Hoyt, *The Invasion Before Normandy–The Secret Battle of Slapton Sands* (Robert Hale Limited, 1985).

Chapter Eight: We Must All Stick Together

Sources:

Lieut. J. F. Murdock Debrief Transcription (document held by Exercise Tiger Trust);

First-hand account of Angelo Crapanzano;

Narrative of Patsy Giacchi—www.mikekemble.com;

Nigel Lewis, *Channel Firing–The Tragedy of Exercise Tiger* (Penguin Books, 1990);

Edwin P. Hoyt, *The Invasion Before Normandy–The Secret Battle of Slapton Sands* (Robert Hale Limited, 1985);

Richard T. Bass, *Exercise Tiger–The D-Day practice landing tragedies uncovered* (Menin House, 2012);

Letters from John A Brown to Marion Irving (held by Exercise Tiger Trust—courtesy of Art and Bev Hughes);

Letter from Ensign Raymond Gosselin to Mrs Hill (held by Exercise Tiger Trust—courtesy of Art and Bev Hughes);

Newspaper article on Edwin James Dobson (held by Exercise Tiger Trust—courtesy of Art and Bev Hughes);

US Army Centre of Military History: WWII documents, VII Exercises;

U.S.N.A.—Trident Scholar project report; no. 221 (1994)—The U.S. Navy in Operation Overlord under the Command of Rear Admiral Alan G. Kirk by Midshipman First Class Troy A. Shoulders, Class of 1994 U.S. Naval Academy, Annapolis, Maryland.

Chapter Nine: It's a Lovely Day Tomorrow

Sources:
First-hand account of Eugene Eckstam;

First-hand account of Angelo Crapanzano;

Account of experiences of Henry Victor Martin Jr., supplied by Suzan Martin Cunningham (daughter);

Memories of D-Day—A Statement by John Robert Lewis Jr. (held by Exercise Tiger Trust);

Nigel Lewis, *Channel Firing–The Tragedy of Exercise Tiger* (Penguin Books, 1990);

Edwin P. Hoyt, *The Invasion Before Normandy–The Secret Battle of Slapton Sands* (Robert Hale Limited, 1985);

Richard T. Bass, *Exercise Tiger–The D-Day practice landing tragedies uncovered* (Menin House, 2012)

Robin Rose-Price and Jean Parnell, *The Land We Left Behind* (Orchard Publications, 2004).

Chapter Ten: Sentimental Journey

Sources:
First-hand account of Eugene Eckstam;

Article written by Ed Panter, LST-289 & 507, Published in LST Scuttlebutt, 2002;

First-hand account of Angelo Crapanzano;

Narrative of Patsy Giacchi—www.mikekemble.com;

Richard T. Bass, *Exercise Tiger–The D-Day practice landing tragedies uncovered* (Menin House, 2012);

German E-boat logs (documents held by Exercise Tiger Trust);

German Comments on Operation, 28 April 1944—Scheveningen (document held by Exercise Tiger Trust);

Memories of D-Day—A Statement by John Robert Lewis Jr. (held by Exercise Tiger Trust).

Index